Gavin Hamilton

# The True Theory of the Subjunctive

The Logic of the Latin Language

Gavin Hamilton

**The True Theory of the Subjunctive**
*The Logic of the Latin Language*

ISBN/EAN: 9783742816733

Manufactured in Europe, USA, Canada, Australia, Japa

Cover: Foto ©Andreas Hilbeck / pixelio.de

Manufactured and distributed by brebook publishing software (www.brebook.com)

Gavin Hamilton

**The True Theory of the Subjunctive**

# THE
# TRUE THEORY OF THE SUBJUNCTIVE,

OR

## THE LOGIC OF THE LATIN LANGUAGE.

BY

## GAVIN HAMILTON,
OF THE ELGIN ACADEMY.

*Apud sapientem argumenta plus quam testes valent.*

EDINBURGH:
OLIVER AND BOYD, TWEEDDALE COURT.
LONDON: SIMPKIN, MARSHALL, AND CO.
1864.

TO

# EDMUND LAW LUSHINGTON, ESQ.,

LATE FELLOW OF TRINITY COLLEGE, CAMBRIDGE,
PROFESSOR OF GREEK IN THE UNIVERSITY OF GLASGOW.

My dear Mr Lushington,

To you, the worthy successor of Sandford, Young, and Moore, in acknowledgment of benefits received as your pupil, which I can never requite, but which I now gladly and gratefully record, and in admiration of your great love of truth, as well as your great learning, I dedicate this work, designed to demonstrate the logic of the Latin language.

With the strongest sentiments of gratitude and regard,

Ever,

Most truly thine,

GAVIN HAMILTON.

# CONTENTS.

|  | PAGE |
|---|---|
| INTRODUCTION, | ix |

### CHAPTER I.
THE GERMAN " ESSENTIAL-PART " THEORY, . . . . 1

### CHAPTER II.
GROTEFEND'S AND FORBIGER'S THEORY OF THE CONDITIONAL, 30

### CHAPTER III.
THE THEORY OF " DEPENDENCE," . . . . . 58

### CHAPTER IV.
THE THEORY OF THE " PREDICATE," . . . . 71

### CHAPTER V.
THE FUNCTION OF *UT*, . . . . . . . 119

### CHAPTER VI.
THE FUNCTION OF *QUUM*, . . . . . . 149

### CHAPTER VII.
THE ESSENTIAL UNITY OF THE SUBJUNCTIVE, . . . 177

# INTRODUCTION.

The Latin language, inasmuch as it is the language of the ancient Romans, the people whose law, literature, and civilisation have influenced to an extent so great, and in a manner so remarkable, the history of the world, can never cease to inspire with feelings of deepest interest, every mind at all imbued with love of liberal culture. But apart altogether from collateral considerations, independently of individual predilections, the singularly logical construction of its sentences, the close connexion and mutual relation of all its constituent clauses, each of which is a formal indication of a step in the train of thought, render its own intrinsic importance very great, as an instrument for developing and disciplining the mind of youth. By no other language is the art of reasoning in written speech so well illustrated. By no other language, ancient or modern, can the science of grammar be so well taught. Accordingly, instead of being admitted to a place in a system or curriculum of study along with other co-ordinate branches, by the wise suffrage of modern opinion it has itself become the basis of a liberal education.

INTRODUCTION.

But the best practical proof of the importance attached to the study of Latin, is the fact that a great preponderance of merit is assigned to it, by many, if not most universities, in competitions for prizes of solid gold. This prevalent practice also supplies the best possible proof of the great attention bestowed alike by teachers and taught on the study of Latin. This practice might also plausibly enough be supposed to supply proofs that Latin is the best understood of all languages, and at this late period of its history nothing in connexion with its structure and genius at once new and true can be produced. As the author is prepared to prove that this, though a common opinion, is not a correct one, he will, in the first place, give it all the advantage that accrues from the most distinguished advocacy. Professor William Young Sellar, after his appointment last year to the chair of Latin in the University of Edinburgh, in his inaugural address, thus spoke with reference to the point at issue:—

"The highest teaching of the classical languages, considered simply as languages, may be said to have advanced as far as it can advance. It may almost be doubted whether, if it were possible, it would be desirable to refine upon it any further."

It would be difficult to conceive a combination of circumstances more effectively calculated to give consideration and circulation to an opinion. The place, period, and personage are all alike remarkable. One educated in the foremost of Scottish schools, where his feats in scholarship were only the forerunner of what was to follow at the university, nominated by the Faculty of Glasgow College to a Snell Exhibition at Oxford, where his academic career was closed by the crowning distinction of an Oriel Fellowship, after having taught in more than one Scottish university, at last appointed to the metropolitan chair of Latin, in the full plenitude and perfection of his intellectual manhood, brings recommendations to the support of an opinion which it would be presumptuous to oppose unless protected by the potent panoply of truth.

Before indicating an opinion opposed to this one, it will be necessary and desirable to see what is the conclusion reached by scholars relative to the moods of the Latin language. This has been laid down distinctly enough by the classical reviewer of the *Athenæum*. The author quotes the judgment all the more readily, that it was delivered against himself in a review of his first work :—

" Surely Mr Hamilton does not suppose he is the first to point out that the indicative mood in Latin is employed to express actual fact, and the subjunctive what is only conceived in the mind. It does not appear to us that he *has advanced beyond this general principle, which is to be met with in any grammar.*"

The author assures the Aristarchus of the *Athenæum* that he " does not suppose himself to be the first to point out that the indicative is the mood of fact, and the subjunctive that of conception ;" but, on the contrary, he claims to be the first to point out *that the expression of fact belongs to the subjunctive as well as to the indicative, and conception to the indicative as well as to the subjunctive.* Without anticipating what is reserved for the body of this work, the seven succeeding sentences, all with different combinations, exhibit *the subjunctive expressing a fact,* and what is more, *without condition, qualification, or reserve.*

Tanto plus virtute militum valuerunt, *ut* decemplicem hostium numerum *profligarent.*—Nep., *Mil.* 5.

Alexander, *quum* Clitum familiarem suum *interemisset,* manus a se vix abstinuit.—Cic., *Tus.,* iv. 37.

Graccho, *priusquam* ex Lucanis *moveret,* sacrificanti, triste prodigium factum est.—Livy, xxv. 16.

*Irae* altis urbibus ultimae
Stetere causae, cur *perirent*
Funditus.—Hor., *Car.,* 1. xvi.

Sunt qui scripta foro *recitent.*
—Hor., *Sat.,* Lib. 1, iv. 75.

Trepidationis aliquantum edebant, *donec* quietem ipse timor *fecisset.*—Livy, xxi. 28.

Mirum, quantum illi viro, nuntianti haec, fidei *fuerit.*—Livy, 1, xvi.

Nor less indubitably is the indicative employed to express a conception.

*Si* quid mea carmina *possunt.*—*Æn.* ix., 446.
*Si* modo in philosophia aliquid *profecimus.*
—Cic., *Of.,* 3, 8.

## INTRODUCTION.

> Quod *si* dolentem nec Phrygius lapis
> Nec purpurarum sidere clarior
> Delinit usus.—Hor., *Car.*, iii. 1.

Now that it has been proved by the most competent authorities, the Latin writers themselves, that "all grammars" have failed to draw the true distinction between the indicative and subjunctive in Latin, the author, with all due deference to Professor Sellar, is strongly disposed to dispute his declaration: —"The highest teaching of the classical languages, considered simply as languages, may be said to have advanced as far as it can advance;" and since, in the ordinary affairs of life, men attach the greatest importance to the difference between a fact and a fancy, he deems it highly "desirable," in opposition to the same authority, to determine when a fact is to be expressed by the subjunctive, and when a fancy is to be expressed by the indicative. Whether it is "possible" to do this or no he refers to the body of this work. The propensity in philology of late has run nearly parallel to that in politics, a propensity to "finality," to "rest and be thankful." Bacon, however, the greatest master of uninspired wisdom, again and again, in the course of his works, as his readers will remember, deprecates the evil effects of a premature system on the progress of science, and dwells on the advantages which will arise from such a partition of the province of knowledge, as to admit the introduction of every improvement.

If the late Professor Zumpt of Berlin was not the first to propound the theory that the "indicative is the mood of actual fact, and the subjunctive the mood of conception," which "is to be met with in any grammar," it is to be found in his well-known work. The celebrity of his name was quite sufficient to give currency to it, to gain for it the stamp of custom, and to obtain for it the sanction of universal use. Bearing, however, less analogy to the genuine gold of truth than to the money of Lycurgus, which did not circulate beyond the bounds of Sparta, it ought never to have left the congenial soil of Germany. It is disfigured to a great degree by the same defects which have characterized all the theories relative to the subjunctive that have emanated from that country. It is characterized by a deliberate disregard of facts. It can scarcely be supposed that Zumpt, who gave laws to Europe on the Latin language, a scholar of the most extraordinary industry, though not of the most extraordinary intellect, was ignorant of the usages of the subjunctive given above. It is more probable that, with the contempt of facts which is characteristic of his countrymen, he constructed a theory which ignores them. Everybody who knows anything about the ideas entertained by Germans relative to the province of philosophy, knows that their catalogue of philosophers contains not the name of Francis Bacon. It is only by courtesy that he can be called a philosopher at all, for he has no intrinsic claim to that august appellation. He deals too much, forsooth, with facts! He ends only where he ought to begin! It is not wonderful that Zumpt should not have risen superior to the perverse notions of his countrymen, who are resolved to be original even at the risk of being wrong; who, starting on a false scent, by every step are led farther astray; who resemble certain birds which never take wing save when the wind is contrary. Their theories are extremely shadowy, for though they have fancy for their soul, they have no fact for their body. The Germans certainly abuse the privilege or license to be fanciful. Although their theories are false in the face of facts, they set their face firmly against the facts. And it is to be regretted that Englishmen have lent their countenance to this barefaced practice. The opinions which have been advanced with so much confidence from Germany have been accepted with no less confiding complacency in the high places of this country. In the British House of Commons, during the debate on the Oxford University Bill, not very long ago, it was thus that Mr Horsman, the Right Hon. the member for Stroud, spoke,—"It was notorious that the Germans surpassed us in classical studies. All the great modern commentators were German; and it was the same in ancient history and philosophy, as Niebuhr's work on Roman History, for instance, was a fountain from which all our knowledge on that subject was drawn. The Germans were now our masters *in every branch of philology*, although this was not the case in the days of Bentley and Porson, who were the equals of any scholar in Europe."

The House, which may be regarded as a representative of public feeling, which *follows rather than forms opinion*, on this occasion fairly fulfilled its function. Mr Gladstone, indeed, as the member for the University, threw the broad shield of his protection over his Alma Mater, the scene of his own youthful triumphs, but his apology seemed scarcely less damaging than the direct accusation of his antagonist. Mr Horsman was not met by any distinct contradiction, so that his representation of the common opinion may be considered correct.

The opinion entertained by Englishmen relative to the scholarship of modern Germans is precisely parallel to the opinion entertained by the soldiers of Cæsar relative to the reputed bravery of the ancient Germans. There is the same exaggeration in each case. Every schoolboy who has read the Commentaries remembers that when the Romans were on the eve of encountering their new enemies they felt far more inclined to flight than to fight. So soon, however, as the two armies met in the field, face to face, it was found that the Germans were not in reality what report represented them to be. They were more remarkable for length of body than strength of arm. The false impression in the case of the ancient Germans was not greater than in the case of the modern Germans. It is not correct to say "that the Germans are our masters in every branch of philology," so far at least as the Latin language is concerned. To use a German phrase, it is a monstrous myth. For a long time the author himself imagined the common opinion to be correct. He supposed that the repute of Zumpt as a scientific grammarian was as well deserved as widely diffused. Nothing was more natural than that he should receive and believe what all other scholars before him had not hesitated to receive and believe. It never occurred to him that Zumpt would either conceive or others believe theories not consistent with the practice of Latin writers. It is quite true that he could not comprehend many parts of these theories, and could not apply successfully any of them, yet with a pardonable, if not praiseworthy diffidence, he attributed this result to his own intellectual infirmity. However, it having at length occurred to him that all the greatest discoveries are obvious to others as well as the originators, he came to the conclusion that these theories were as untrue as they were unintelligible. This conclusion is not without a parallel. The late Francis Horner thus writes in his Memoirs,—" The discovery that I did not understand Adam Smith, led me to doubt whether he understood himself, and I thought I saw that the price of labour was the same sort of thing as any other commodity."

Mr Horner, who possessed to an extraordinary extent and in admirable equipoise a combination of those conditions which produce the successful thinker,—a fine moral sense, extreme conscientiousness, a profound love of truth, and keen intellectual vision,—by long meditation, had thoroughly mastered his subject, and therefore had fairly purchased the right to use great plainness of speech. His mental organization was as remarkable for the absence of indifference or indolence as intellectual impotence. Convinced of the invincibility of the pure force of truth, conscious of the possession of truth on his own side, he exhibited none of that reluctance to reason which places its reliance on authority, and takes ready refuge in submission to a conventional supremacy. He never offered up the costly sacrifice of independent judgment to mere authority. He believed nothing but what it was impossible to doubt, and what would be a contradiction to deny. He approached his subject imbued with the true Baconian spirit, exhibiting all the freedom of inquiry and criticism which the law of modern progress demands. His example illustrated the action of that law of progress which transfers the sceptre from authority based on conventional considerations to argument based on reason. His example also indicated the true difference between science which shows things as they are, and philosophy which sees things as they seem, and proved that the misconceptions of philosophy, when subjected to the scrutiny of science, melt like mist before the midday sun, not a vestige remaining, but vanishing like visions of the night. Mr Horner's motto was,—

*Rimari,* non *mirari,* vera est sapientia.

It would have been better if Englishmen, following the example of Mr Horner rather than Mr Horsman, after acquainting themselves with the results of modern German speculation in Latin philology, instead of acquiescing in and admiring them, had, before trusting them, tested them by the touchstone of reason. The author maintains that the Latin philological theories of Germany, looming large in the distance, have been magnified by its mist beyond their deserts, and been blown into circulation by the breath of credulity. But they no less surely shall burst before the sharp and piercing blast of truth. The author, so far from believing with Mr Horsman that the Germans are our "masters in every branch of philology," believes, Diogenes-like, so far at least as Latin is concerned, that they only stand between the sun of truth and the students of the Latin language, and that it is reasonable that they should be requested to stand aside. Accordingly, declining to look at Latin through German spectacles, the author has used his own unaided sight in the study of Roman writers. The mind, moreover, is more strengthened by the warmth of its own independent exercise than by foreign clothes. To compare great things with small, the scientific grammarian, unlike the Marquis Cornwallis, who, as successor to Lord Wellesley, Governor-General of India, said to Mr Addington, "that nothing had been left for him to do," needs not to make the same complaint. It has been already seen in this Introduction, that on a primary and paramount point of Latin syntax, the difference between the indicative and subjunctive, the decision of Zumpt—the Ζίυς μέγας of the classical Olympus, οὗ κράτος ἰστὶ μέγιστον is both erroneous and defective. To Zumpt's supposition, which no man can prove, the author has opposed a whole host of facts from the Roman writers which prove themselves. Fortunately for the fate of the Latin language and the interests of education, the question is removed altogether from the region of speculation to that of demonstration. It is not a question of conventionalities, but of realities. In theology and philosophy there are many questions on which it is not possible to attain, but only to approximate toward certainty. In many cases proof is not possible, but only a preponderance of probability. It is not so here. The right decision of the point at issue rests on the rock of truth, though Zumpt's decision rests only on the sand of supposition. It was either based on a deliberate disregard of facts, as already stated, or founded on a partial and accidental circumstance, instead of a universal and essential principle. Such as it is, it is neither sound nor profound. It is an opinion which is not the offspring of observation. Zumpt, in adopting it, assumed the office of an advocate before exercising the office of a philosopher. But to look for flaws in the argument of a German Latin philologist, is to look for holes in a sieve. He is usually, if not uniformly, lame in his logic, and breaks down, ere, like a skilful explorer, he reaches the terminus of truth.

The name of Kruger in Germany, as a Latin philologist, enjoys a repute second only to that of Zumpt. His System of Latin Syntax was so highly prized by the late Mr Kerchever Arnold, as to be incorporated bodily in his well-known treatise, Part I. It was regarded, no doubt, as a masterpiece of art, and as a model for imitation. In it are to be found thirty solemn rules for the subjunctive, *i.e.*, thirty different rules for the same uniform result! If the value of a system is to be determined by its length, if worth is to be estimated by weight, if multitude rather than magnitude is an index of value, this is assuredly one of the most valuable systems ever given to the world. Unity, however, and simplicity have always been the surest tests of truth. Accordingly, a scientific system of syntax will aim at improving the quality, rather than increasing the quantity of rules, will respect character, rather than number. It ought, moreover, in reducing the number of rules, to show their resemblance to each other, since they all refer to the same result. The rules, however, of Kruger, bear no more resemblance to each other than to the angle of polarization. Nor is there any reason given for any rule. Rules without reasons are like walls without windows. To offer a rule without a reason to a student of language, is to give a stone and not bread. A rule without a reason encumbers the understanding without enriching it. The noble fabric of the Latin language, fashioned by master-hands, was so framed that a reason may readily be rendered for all its rules, and a clear and close relationship be proved between them. Latin syntax is not a field for the exercise of arbitrary taste, but a symmetrical system subject to the great laws of logic. Its most secret recesses may be traversed, not in the shadowy twilight of random conjecture and arbitrary arrangement, but in the full, broad, clear light of scientific demonstration. It is a cosmos, not a chaos. Faith in its laws firmly rests on reason. There being but *one form* for the Latin subjunctive, the true logical *à priori* conception regarding it would be, that the Latin writers in employing it, whatever might be its accompanying verbal combinations, employed it to express *one idea*. This is the dictate of common sense. But the notion entertained regarding it by all scholars, British and European, up to this day, presents an anomaly, to which no parallel is to be found in philosophy or science. There is one usage of the indicative, imperative, infinitive, respectively, how, then, in the name of common sense, can there be thirty different usages of the subjunctive? Long ere the author could demonstrate it, he believed that there must be an essential unity underlying all the usages of the subjunctive, that, however apparently remote, they must all be really related to each other. Careful and constant study of the Latin writers at last furnished him with case after case, in which a common characteristic made the chain of coincidence complete. In the last chapter of this work, the summary of the results of his investigations contains a list of more than thirty usages of the subjunctive, which all express one common idea. This summary the author begs to confront with the German system of thirty different rules for one and the same result. He has been for some time anxious to discover a theory to which boys with logical heads might listen without laughter.

The selection by Mr Horsman of one German name for special commendation, to the rejection of others, is singularly significant. Seldom, indeed, has scholarship or science been enriched by intellectual conquests more solid or more splendid than those imperishably associated with the noble name of Niebuhr. No eulogium from any quarter whatever could make his repute more certain or conspicuous, and any encomium here, would only be as the addition of an atom to the Alps or the Andes. But the author believes that the exaggerated opinion of German scholarship owes its origin in a great measure to the extraordinary influence of the historian of Rome. It is scarcely too much to say that the publication of his great work, which serves as a historical milestone to mark the progress of human speculation, and the ascendancy of German influence in philology, stand related to each other as cause and effect. Everything else that has subsequently appeared in connexion with his name has tended to preserve and perpetuate the original impression. The portrait prefixed to his lectures on *Roman History* presents a countenance eloquent of everything that is excellent in man. His

*Life* and *Letters* exhibit a character which charms by its consistency and completeness. Like the Church of St Peter at Rome, it strikes the spectator by its symmetry rather than its size. Each of his intellectual faculties, however, was projected on a scale so extraordinary as to have supplied the staple for several ordinary reputations. His marvellous memory in the mastery of languages may sustain a comparison with any in ancient, mediæval, or modern times, with Mithridates, Pico Mirandola, or the late Dr Mill. Perhaps only Cardinal Mezzofanti might be considered his superior, who, "though he could speak in any language, could say nothing in any." His judgment is so sure that his readers almost forget that he is a German. He is so sensible and practical, so familiar with their history, now discussing the constitution of the East India Company, now declaiming on the judicial murder of Admiral Byng, that Englishmen might claim him as a compatriot. A Frenchman in describing his nationality would represent Fortune as having made a mistake in making him a German. His invention has received a most splendid illustration in the reconstruction of the ancient annals of Rome, in the re-adjustment of the relation between the mythological and historical element, in the demarcation of the line, deep, broad, and strong, which separates the firm land of fact from the shadowy domain of fiction. Not the binder of sheaves, which other men have reaped, his investigations have won for him a front place among the foremost men of all time; those who have extended the empire of human knowledge, who have made successful inroads on the domains of the unknown, who have diminished the disproportion between the discovered and the undiscovered, who win the homage of history, are an honour to humanity:—

Quique sui memores alios fecere merendo.

Sobriety and sagacity are the basis on which are built his best and most brilliant qualities. Under the admirably adjusted action of these there was no room for the fantastic flights of fancy in which his countrymen are so apt to indulge. His powerful imagination, so essential to the perfection of the historic faculty, was kept in check by the presence of other co-ordinate powers, which, by their peculiar combination, received and reflected mutual lustre. The reflected light of this great luminary still shines in the literary firmament, long after it has disappeared from sight. This is the torch from which so many tapers have taken fire and burned with borrowed light. All German scholars, however, are not Niebuhrs. Neither Zumpt nor Kruger is a Niebuhr. There can be no second Niebuhr any more than there can be a second Napoleon.

Before closing this Introduction, the author desires to tender his most grateful acknowledgments to Professor Hepworth Thomson, of the University of Cambridge, the able editor of Archer Butler, and one of Her Majesty's Commissioners for Public Schools, for an analysis of a portion of his first treatise, of which he has availed himself in the second chapter of the present work. He has also to thank him for a reference to a paper in the Philological Museum by Professor Malden, on the Subjunctive. He did not, however, consult this publication, as he felt inclined to follow out the investigations he had instituted to an independent issue.

With equally genuine gratitude, acknowledgments are made to Professor Conington of the University of Oxford, for his great courtesy in supplying the emendations of the commentators in the Bodleian Library, on a disputed passage in Livy.

One word or two are due to reviewers. The author having ventured in his first treatise for the first time to oppose opinions, which till then were considered as orthodox as they were old, knowing, as Swift hath said, "that the receipt for a wise man is agreeing with what any one may say," and knowing, as the Dean of St Patrick hath also said :—

>    Truth and censure with a tether,
>    By Fate are always linked together:

He quoted these brave lines in his preface :—

>    Caedimus inque vicem praebemus crura sagittis.

So far from dreading or deprecating criticism, there was nothing which he desired more. And it happened actually as he had anticipated. With one solitary exception, indeed, none of the critics so much as even attempted to answer arguments, but they engaged in the less difficult and more delightful exercise of abusing their author. The simple question which a wise and just man would have asked, is this, are the new opinions now propounded, true? But instead of this, with whatever was irrelevant to the main issue they interfered. One critic said, "he has had the bad taste to differ with those who have gone before him." If there is any force, truth, or even taste in this censure, then it follows that Harvey, who discovered and demonstrated the circulation of the blood, was a man of bad taste, since his predecessors maintained that the bloodvessels were filled with air. In like manner, according to this sapient sage, since the ruins round about had to be removed, ere the edifice of St Paul's could be reared, Sir Christopher Wren must have been a man of bad taste. Another critic complains of the style. A good horse cannot have a bad colour. No writer who can make out that what he says is both new and true, can have a bad style. A third censures the "assumption." It has been the author's aim always to argue, never to assume. He has never asked his readers to *approve*, what he himself has failed to *prove*. A fourth complains that the whole work is a "series of attacks." The author has attacked no man, although he has attacked the opinions of many. There is a great difference. He who does the former, lights a firebrand; he who does the latter, burns incense at the altar of truth. A fifth, after two columns of consistent and persistent misrepresentation, accuses the author of misrepresenting Grotefend and Zumpt. This is just as ludicrous as if the editor of a newspaper were to complain of bearing false witness against a neighbour, or the Gracchi were to complain of sedition, or Satan were to reprove sin, or a man who was in the habit of beating his wife were to complain of cruelty to animals. Sterne says, "when a man has firmly fixed on his subject, then for a text, Cappadocia, Pontus and Asia, Phrygia and Pamphylia, is as good as any in the Bible." Most of these critics, members of the teaching profession, but neither the highest nor most honourable, seeking to gratify their own "safe malignity," as Earl Russell has fitly phrased it, behind the shield of anonymous journalism, by seizing such pretexts enumerated above,—a device which cannot deceive twice,—have laboured hard to justify it to others. So it has always been. Scientific readers will remember that Crosse the electrician read some papers at the British Association in Bristol, 1836, which at once rendered him famous. By the fire of genius he had forged a link in science, which all his forerunners had failed to find. Forthwith, a company of sciolists, who had cultivated the same or similar pursuits, raised a cry through the press, in which the voice of reason, conscience, and justice, was drowned. They revenged themselves by reviling the man they could not rival. But they only precipitated what they could neither prevent nor postpone. The case of Crosse proves that the press with all its power, can neither give nor take away true fame. Truth, with time, is a match for any two. The stumbling-blocks which are thrown in its way, it turns into stepping-stones to its triumph. Whoever has truth on his side can venture to oppose and overcome any odds. With no other weapon could the author have ventured to oppose or overcome the authority of Zumpt, Madvig, Donaldson, and Parr, in his solution of the problem of the subjunctive. He will not say that critics will find it hard to argue with him, but he will say with Socrates of old, "it is hard, O Agathon, to argue with the truth."

The Academy, Elgin,
8th November 1864.

## CHAPTER I.

### THE GERMAN "ESSENTIAL-PART THEORY."

But for its contravention by others, the author would not have deemed it necessary or even desirable to revert to his principle of specific predication. The partiality peculiar to intellectual paternity, pardonable, perhaps, if not praiseworthy, would have predisposed him to believe that nothing more was needed to establish its truth. What, however, appears to one's own partiality superfluous in the way of proof, to others often appears not even sufficient. In the additional proofs now adduced, it is hoped there may be sufficient force to convince those who are or were disposed to doubt, though the author's own conviction cannot be stronger than when his principle was first propounded.

A most distinguished University Professor, who would be regarded by many as the highest authority in England on the subject in question, thus writes in a communication addressed to the author: "I am unable to see the need of your rule.—Qui is not only used indefinitely with respect to persons, but also to places and periods." Fortune has effected a combination of circumstances peculiarly favourable for the defence of this rule thus referred to by the learned Professor. A critique, which appeared in the Edinburgh (Daily) Review, condemning the principle of specific predication, without qualification, limitation, or reserve, affords a fit opportunity of defending it in detail. The defence will be the more easy, conducted as it is against an assault made by the agency of assertions and arguments equally inaccurate. The very title of the book, which contains the principle in question, could not escape the censure of the critic. Thus he commences operations,—" We doubt if the title of this work gives a fair idea of the contents of the book. Mr Hamilton has discussed no theory that is in any special way German. What he has done may be summed up thus:—He has taken up detached passages in three school-books, two of which were translations from the German, and he has attacked these passages as if they had contained some monstrous grammatical heresies." Let the accuracy of the latter part of this statement be tested. The treatise containing the "essential-part theory" which the author impugned, and to which he referred, specifying edition and page, is thus entitled by its publishers, Longman & Co., A Grammar of the Latin Language, by C. G. Zumpt, Professor in the University, and Member of the Royal Academy of Berlin, Translated from the Ninth Edition of the Original, and Adapted to the Use of English Students, by Leonhard Schmitz, Ph.D., F.R.S.E., Rector of the High School of Edinburgh. A book described by its title-page as adapted for "students" cannot truly be called a "school-book." Moreover, the publishers issued an abridgment of this work for the "use of schools." The critic would have done better not to have made any remark at all on this point. A weak case could not have been strengthened, even if the statement thus hazarded had been actually correct, and a strong case could not fail to have been weakened by a statement thus proved to be incorrect. Nor is the critic's argument more correct than his assertion. He does not seem to have seen that, even if Professor Zumpt's Latin Grammar had been a school-book, the inference thence to be drawn is all the more favourable to the author. If errors exist in school-books, the sooner they are exposed and eradicated, the greater will be the gain of schools. Now, let the former part of the extract quoted above be considered,—" Mr Hamilton has discussed no theory that is in any special way German." While accuracy in every case is desirable in those who profess to perform the part of instructors, it is especially necessary in the case of those who assume to themselves the part of instructing instructors. Error in such a case, whether arising from ignorance, or the misrepresentation of facts, or the suppression of facts, is equally reprehensible. The extract just quoted contains a statement directly contradictory of a writer, who ventures to say of himself, that he was careful to ascertain the accuracy of his statements. The statement is purely arbitrary, advanced by an anonymous writer, without even an attempt to support it by a citation of evidence. There are those, the owners of distinguished names, whose simple signature enables them to dispense with the detailed formality of proof. With them, in matters of fact, to state is to substantiate; in matters of opinion, to state is to demonstrate. This peculiarity, however, does not pertain to anonymous scribes. With them, proof is indispensable. A buyer with name unknown must produce his gold. A stranger to gain belief must produce his credentials. In the ordinary affairs of life, men don't believe without a reason, or trust without security. This reviewer, however, has drawn largely on the credulity of his readers. His draft, therefore, deserves to be dishonoured. He has said that the theory in question "is in no special way German." Here is the proof that it is. The late Professor Zumpt of Berlin, in the edition quoted above, thus wrote:—" (A) The subjunctive is used in clauses where they form an essential part of the statement implied in the accusative with the infinitive (p. 392). (B) Clauses introduced into a proposition which is expressed by the subjunctive, are likewise in the subjunctive when they are to be considered as an essential part of the leading proposition (p. 393). Memoria erat tanta (Hortensius) quantam in nullo cognovisse me arbitror, *ut, quæ secum commentatus esset*, ea sine scripto verbis eisdem redderet, *quibus cogitavisset*. Cic., *Brut.* 88. The same rule and the same example also occur in Kenrick's edition of Zumpt. The theory thus was not hastily adopted or hastily abandoned by its author. It was next adopted by Kruger, another distinguished German grammarian, who also appropriated the well-known example—Memoria erat tanta (Hortensius), etc. Kruger says (in his Treatise on the Subjunctive),—" Finally, those relative clauses which are incorporated in a sentence whose verb is in the subjunctive, or in a clause consisting of the accusative with the infinitive (which, as forming the object of some intellectual activity, denotes something thought or conceived), usually have their verb in the subjunctive, even when they express what might be conceived as independent of any body's thought. By the *subjunctive* the relative clause is more *thoroughly incorporated* with the other sentence as a *part* of the *whole thought*." Dr Schmitz, himself a German, in his grammar, p. 269, adopts the theory of his countrymen, and quotes the very same example in support of it—Memoria erat tanta (Hortensius), etc. Here, then, are three German treatises of the highest authority, which contain the "essential-part theory." On the other hand, let the three Scottish treatises by Maclure, Carson, and Melvin, be examined from beginning to end, and not one word will be found relative to the "essential-part theory." It is thus essentially a German theory. It is true that the theory appears in the treatise of Professor Madvig of Copenhagen, p. 318, but the old example—Memoria erat tanta (Hortensius), etc., betrays the German source. It also appears in a Latin form in Dr Kennedy's (of Shrewsbury) Latin grammar, Relativum vel conjunctio, quum subordinatur subjunctivo, subjunctivum regit, coupled, of course, with the invariable and indispensable German adjunct, Memoria erat tanta (Hortensius), etc., p. 129, sixth edition. So much for the reviewer's bare assertion, "the theory is not in any special way German."

It is now time to consider the reviewer's defence of the theory. It will be seen that there is a close affinity between the character of his assertions and of his arguments. His arguments are as inconclusive as his assertions are inaccurate. He says, "The passage in Zumpt's grammar attacked is as follows:—'The subjunctive mood is used with clauses inserted in the construction of the accusative with the infinitive, when they are to express the thoughts or words of the person spoken of, *or* when they form an *essential part of the statement implied in the accusative with the infinitive.*'" Mr Hamilton's strength is spent on an attempt to show that the portion in *italics* is wrong. It is very likely that if he had spent as much time in trying to comprehend Zumpt's statements as he has spent on writing against one small portion of them, he would never have made the attack. Zumpt first lays down the general principle which Mr Hamilton takes no notice of, "The subjunctive is used in propositions which are introduced into others, after relative pronouns and conjunctions, when these propositions express the thoughts or words of another person. (In many cases they are the thoughts or words of the speaker himself; but he then speaks of himself as of a third person).

To make this general rule more clear, we shall distinguish the various cases in which such clauses are inserted!" It was in pure compassion to the reader that the author did not quote more of the context from Zumpt, and not from any desire or design to misrepresent Zumpt. He had no desire to do so, for he had stated in the preface to his original work, "The author knows that he has not misrepresented the scholars whose opinions have been impugned in these pages; he believes he has not misunderstood them," much less had he any design to misrepresent Zumpt for the sake of a temporary triumph, for he knew well that the design would have been discovered and denounced as it deserved. The author makes the reviewer very welcome to what he thinks should have been extracted in connexion with the theory assailed. It is with great pleasure that it has been here re-extracted.

When Zumpt wrote the words, "The subjunctive is used with clauses inserted in the construction of the accusative with the infinitive, when they are to express the thoughts or words of the person spoken of, or when they form an essential part of the statement implied in the accusative with the infinitive," he either intended to include in the latter part of the rule a class of sentences different and distinct from the class included by the first part of the rule, or the words form a conglomeration of unmeaning tautology. If there could have been any reasonable doubt as to the meaning of Zumpt, that doubt would have been removed by the two sentences which the grammarian himself adduces in illustration of his rule. The first is, Socrates dicere solebat, omnes in eo quod scirent, satis esse eloquentes.—Cic., *de Orat.*, i. 14. This clearly enough illustrates the first part of the rule. The second sentence, with equal clearness, illustrates the second part of the rule. Mos est Athenis, laudari in concione eos, qui sint in prœliis interfecti.—Cic., *Orat.*, 44. That is to say, the subjunctive qui—interfecti sint is used, because it *forms an essential part of the statement implied in the accusative with the infinitive.* Such is the interpretation which the author originally put on Zumpt's rule, and to it he still adheres. Here, on the other hand, is the reviewer's representation of the rule. "Zumpt there states, when a relative, *or such like clause*, is so essential to the reported thought or speech expressed by the accusative with the infinitive, that it is really to be regarded as part of the thought, then it is to be placed with the subjunctive." This honourable, high-minded, chivalrous critic, who was horrified at the omissions of others, not only omits the words of Zumpt, but adds others of his own, and then adds, "taken in its connexion, Zumpt's *statement can mean nothing else.* No scholar will for a moment hesitate as to this rule. Zumpt may be wrong in adducing as examples of this rule passages which are examples of some others. But the rule itself is unquestionable. We do not think that Zumpt is happy in all his examples, but he is correct in most."

Two thoughts suggest themselves in connexion with the latter part of this extract. The first is, it is somewhat strange that the reviewer, anxious that the author should never be right, goes so far as to say that Zumpt ever was wrong. The second thought is, if Zumpt "was wrong in his examples," it is strange that the reviewer did not embrace the opportunity thus offered of adducing correct examples. The whole world of Latin literature was all before him, but he does not so much as choose a single example. He might have done for Zumpt what Coke did for Littleton, what Dumont did for Bentham, what Sir William Hamilton did for Reid. But he has done nothing at all. He does not even venture to cite a single example from Zumpt himself, even though he alleges "that most of his examples are correct." The truth of a rule can only be inferred from a large induction of examples; and if a grammarian expects others to believe in the truth of his rule, he is bound to cite evidence in support of it. This has been the uniform usage of grammarians ever since philology has assumed the shape of a formal science. An example has always been deemed the best explanation. Bacon himself says that an illustration gives a quicker and deeper impression than an argument. Sterne says that an illustration, though not a syllogism, yet, like wiping a looking-glass, makes one see much better. The reviewer, however, has got a new theory, but far from being as true as it is new. He seems to think that it is the part of grammarians to give laws to language arbitrarily, whereas language, if only allowed freedom to speak, lays down laws for itself. He declares the rule to be "correct," and though he considers "most of the examples correct," he fails to produce a single one of them. Every one of these examples elsewhere the author has questioned, yet the reviewer considers the rule "unquestionable." What the reviewer means by this "rule" may be doubtful. If he means by this "rule" the rule which he himself has compiled, partly by omitting the words of Zumpt, partly by interpolating his own, the author declines to pronounce on the value or truth of the rule, and rests satisfied with "hesitating as to the correctness" of this strange principle or plan of constructing rules. If he means, on the other hand, by this "rule" the plain words of Zumpt, then, at the risk of being "considered no scholar," he "hesitates as to the correctness" of this rule. The reviewer, after giving his own paraphrase or perversion of Zumpt's rule, says, "Taken in its connexion, Zumpt's statement can mean nothing else." He also, as quoted above, said, when speaking of the author, "It is very likely that if he had spent as much time in trying to comprehend Zumpt's statements as he has spent on writing against one small portion of them, he would never have made the attack."

This charge of "not comprehending" Zumpt ought not to have been made on slight grounds. It could only be justified by being based on evidence clear and convincing. But the reviewer here, as elsewhere throughout, in perfect consistency with his practice, presumes everything, proves nothing. If the author has "not comprehended" Zumpt, then it follows that Kruger, a German of the highest eminence as a classical scholar, is liable to the same charge. Kruger, in his treatise on the subjunctive, says, "Finally, those relative clauses which are incorporated in a sentence whose verb is in the subjunctive, or in a clause consisting of the accusative with infinitive (which, as forming the object of some intellectual activity, denotes something thought or conceived), usually have their verb in the subjunctive, *even when they express what might be conceived as independent of any body's thought*. By the subjunctive the relative clause is more thoroughly incorporated with the other sentence as part of the whole thought." The very first word, "Finally," proves that a new class of sentences, different and distinct from any previously considered, is to be introduced; and by employing the words, "*even when they express what might be conceived as independent of any body's thought,*" Kruger expressly excludes "the general principle" which the reviewer censures the author for "taking no notice of;" and, to crown all, Kruger cites, in support of the rule, Zumpt's own example,—Erat Hortensio memoria tanta, etc. This citation from Kruger might have served as a sufficient and satisfactory refutation of the charge of not "comprehending Zumpt's statements;" however, as the imputation of ignorance of German classical literature to the author, is a favourite weapon of offence with the reviewer, one other citation must be made, more conclusive and more decisive still. There can be no one so ignorant or so ill disposed as to impute ignorance either of the English or German language to Dr Schmitz. That learned gentleman is the translator of Zumpt. In that capacity he was responsible only for the meaning of Zumpt, not for the value or the truth of his theories. But Dr Schmitz has published a Latin grammar of his own in this country. At p. 269 of that treatise, he says, "The subjunctive is used in all clauses introduced into a dependent clause either by a relative pronoun or a conjunction, provided they form an integral part of it. By a dependent clause is meant one expressed by the accusative with the infinitive, or having its verb in the subjunctive. A clause forming an integral part of such a sentence is absolutely necessary, and without it, the whole does not and cannot convey a distinct meaning:—"In Hortensio memoria tanta fuit, ut, quæ secum commentatus esset, ea sine scripto verbis eisdem redderet; here quæ secum commentatus esset forms an inseparable part of the clause introduced by ut." Dr Schmitz himself takes no more notice of Zumpt's "general principle" than the author does. Hence, if the author, as the reviewer alleges, "has not comprehended Zumpt's statements," it follows that Dr Schmitz and Kruger have done the same; and though the treatises of these scholars have long been before the world, yet the reviewer, with all his zeal for Zumpt, has never censured them for "not comprehending the statement" of that celebrated grammarian.

The language of Dr Schmitz is so express as to exclude even the existence of doubt. Not only does he adopt to the full the theory of Zumpt, without limitation, qualification, or reserve, and employ that illustration in support of it which has been so great a favourite with the followers of Zumpt, but he expressly specifies the very clause which he cousiders a proof of the truth of the rule,—" In Hortensio memoria tanta fuit, ut, quæ secum commentatus esset, ea sine scripto verbis eisdem redderet; *here quæ secum commentatus esset forms an inseparable part of the clause introduced by ut.*"

The evidence which the author elsewhere has cited in contravention of this theory, is limited in amount, and negative rather than positive in character. Subsequent reading has supplied him with additional evidence, so positive and direct, as, it is hoped, will be sufficient to complete the process of proof. It is here maintained that the clause introduced by ut ... redderet—exercises no influence whatever on the incorporated subjunctive quæ commentatus esset. The conjunction *ut* is a mere accident, and not an essential at all in the production of the result at issue. Zumpt, and the eminent scholars who have followed him so faithfully, have confounded an accidental concomitant with an essential cause.

Before proceeding with the process of positive proof, it has been deemed desirable to cite one or two passages, which first raise grave doubts as to the infallibility of the German principle of interpreting incorporated clauses, and then supply the key to their true explanation. The first passage is taken from Livy, i. 36, Auguriis certe sacerdotioque augurum tantus honos accessit, ut nihil belli domique *postea*, nisi auspicato, gereretur; concilia populi, exercitus vocati; summa rerum, ubi aves non admisissent, dirimerentur. "So great consideration accrued to divination at least, and the college of soothsayers, that nothing afterwards during war or peace was transacted without consulting the omens; the assemblies of the people, the summoning of armies, the most important concerns of the state were put off, *whenever* the birds had not given their sanction." In the above Latin sentence, there is a clause with ut and the subjunctive—ut dirimerentur—the same tense as in the notorious—ut ea sine scripto redderet—followed by an incorporated clause—ubi aves non admisissent—the same tense also as in the notorious—quæ secum commentatus esset. Livy, in this sentence, is writing about the administration of Ancus, and in employing the term *postea*, he embraces a period extending from the time of Ancus to his own time, and hence no specific occasion is indicated by the tense in—ubi aves non admisissent, —but the observance of a custom recurring from time to time throughout the whole of that period. The use of the subjunctive—ubi admisissent—is therefore quite irrespective and independent of the preceding ut dirimerentur.

A similar passage, combining the same conditions, and pointing to the same conclusion, occurs in Nepos, —Quare fiebat, *ut* oculos omnium, *quotiescunque* in publicum *prodisset, ad se converteret*, neque ei par quisquam in civitate poneretur.—*Alcib.* 3.

These two sentences show that the mood of the incorporated clause is influenced by the nature of the predication, and by nothing else. Should it be objected, that in the cases just cited, *uti* and *quotiescunque* are relative adverbs, but not relatives, and therefore not strictly parallel to the clauses cited by Zumpt and his followers, another step in the process of proof has only to be taken.

The incorporated clause is by no means always in the subjunctive. The indicative is as common as the subjunctive, and since *ut* precedes the incorporated indicative as well as the incorporated subjunctive, it cannot be the cause of the latter. The fact is, the one mood or the other is employed according to circumstances. When a writer wishes to make a predication indefinite as to time or place, he employs the subjunctive; but, on the other hand, when he wishes to make a predication definite as to time or place, he employs the indicative.

Let examples of the former case be given—an incorporated subjunctive clause.

The selection comprises specimens from very various writers, proving that the principle of predication indefinite and definite, was not confined to one writer, but common to all.

In his life of Cimon, chap. iv., Nepos says,—*Quotidie sic cœna ei coquebatur, ut quos invocatos vidisset, omnes in foro devocaret.* "Every day dinner was prepared for him on such a scale as to enable him to ask all to partake of it, whom he had seen without an invitation in the market-place." It would be impossible for language to indicate more clearly than this passage does, a custom (quotidie—quos vidisset) indefinitely observed, in contradistinction to a single specific act on a particular day. Compare, or rather contrast, with this sentence the following from the same writer:—*Sed hic plura persequi cum magnitudo voluminis prohibet, tum festinatio, ut, quæ exorsus sum, explicem.* "But both the size of my treatise and haste to narrate what I have undertaken, prevent me from pursuing this theme at greater length." The incorporated clause—quæ orsus sum—contains an indicative, even though preceded by ut, because it points to a specific occasion, when Nepos was tracing the last line of his Preface, and about to trace the first of the life of Miltiades.

Further, from the same writer, Atticus, ii., *Cum enim versuram facere publice necesse esset, neque ejus conditionem aequam haberent, semper se interposuit, atque ita, ut neque usuram unquam ab iis acceperit, neque longius, quam dictum esset eos debere passus sit.* "For when it was required to contract a loan in name of the state, and they could not effect it on fair terms, he *always* interfered, and in such a way, as never either to take interest from them, or to allow them to be in debt longer than had been stipulated." The word *semper* in the Latin version of this sentence proves that the stipulation indicated by the incorporated subjunctive—quam dictum esset—was not limited to one specific occasion, but was a series of stipulations recurring from time to time.

The next illustrative instance is taken from Cæsar, *De Bello Gal.* Horum adventu tanta rerum commutatio est facta, ut nostri etiam qui vulneribus confecti *procubuissent* (at any period whatever during the battle) scutis innixi, prœlium redintegrarent.

So great a change of affairs took place at the arrival of these, that even our men who had fallen prostrate, overpowered with wounds, renewed the combat.—Lib. ii. 27.

There is a passage in Livy, known to every scholar, so strikingly similar to that just quoted, both in syntax and in sentiment, and so completely confirmatory of this principle of indefinite predication, that it ought to be here quoted. Nec qui paululum titubassent (perhaps 50 or 100 times in different places) hærere afflicti vestigio suo possent. Livii, Lib. xxi.-xxxv. Nor could those, who had stumbled a little, when once dashed down on the ground, recover their footing.

As an instance of precise predication from Cæsar, the following passage may be selected :—Ipse interim in colle medio triplicem aciem instruxit legionum quatuor veteranarum, ita, *ut* supra se in summo jugo duas legiones, *quas* in Gallia citeriore *proxime conscripserat*, et omnia auxilia *collocaret*. Lib. i. xxiv. *De Bel. Gal.* In the meantime, he drew up in person his four veteran legions in three lines on the middle of the hill, in such a way as to post above himself on the top of the ridge, the two legions, which he had lately levied in Hither Gaul.

Here in the clause—quas in Gallia proxime conscripserat—there is a specific reference to a place and point of time; hence the indicative is used, in spite of *ut* preceding.

There is also a considerable resemblance between the two following passages, one from Livy, the other from Cicero:—Tantusque ardor fuit, *ut* eodem impetu, *quo fuderant* hostem, Romani castra caperent. Hoc modo ad lacum Regillum pugnatum est. Livii, ii. 20. And so great was the enthusiasm engendered, that the Romans took the camp at the same charge with which they had routed the foe.

The other passage, which is from Cicero, is as follows:—Solent hoc boni imperatores facere, quum proelium committunt, *ut* in eo loco, *quo* fugam hostium fore *arbitrentur*, milites collocent, in quos, si qui ex acie fugerint, de improviso incidant. *Orat. pro Sex. Ros. Amer.* 52. Skilful commanders, when giving battle, are wont to do this; to post their men on that ground, where they think the enemy will flee, on whom, if any escape from the scene of action, they may fall unawares.

In each of these sentences, there is an incorporated

clause preceded by *ut*, and containing a predication relative to soldiers; but in the one the predication is definite as to time and place, in the other the predication is indefinite, and the difference is aptly expressed by a difference of mood—quo (lake of Regillus) fuderant hostem—quo (any place whatever) fugam hostium fore arbitrentur.

Finally, under this head, there remains to be quoted from Livy a passage, definite with respect to all the particulars of persons, place, and point of time, made, of course, by the indicative, on which the preceding clause with *ut* exercises as much influence as it does on a subjunctive under similar circumstances, *i.e.*, nothing at all.

Ibi quum velut septos montium altitudo teneret Gallos, circumspectarentque quanam per juncta coelo juga in alium orbem terrarum transirent, religio etiam tenuit, quod allatum est advenas, quærentes agrum, ab Salyum gente oppugnari. Massilienses erant hi, navibus a Phocæa profecti. Id Galli fortunæ suæ omen rati adjuvere, *ut, quem primum in terram egressi occupaverant,* communirent.

There, when the height of the mountains was keeping the Gauls hemmed in as it were, and they were looking round to see by what route they might cross over ridges rising to the heavens, to the other side of the globe, a religious scruple also arrested their course, because intelligence was brought that strangers in quest of a settlement were being besieged by the nation of the Salyans. These were the inhabitants of Marseilles, who had left Phocæa by sea. The Gauls believing that to be an augury of their own success, lent them their help in fortifying the place which they had first seized on their landing,—being covered with wide extended forests. Lib. v. xxxiv.

Here is the principle of precise predication exemplified in all its particulars,—persons—Massilienses—point of time—primum—place—locum patentibus sylvis. The clause quem occupaverant is as much a part of the entire statement, as if it had contained the subjunctive. In Livy's opinion, at least, it is an "essential part of the entire statement," otherwise it could not have been there.

Thus far has this argument been maintained, that an incorporated clause with a subjunctive is entirely independent of a preceding clause with *ut* and the subjunctive, inasmuch as the indicative is found as frequently in the same place. The choice of the mood is determined solely by the nature of the predication. The subjunctive is used when the predication is indefinite; the indicative is used, on the other hand, when the predication is definite.

There is a second argument which may be raised with reference to this peculiar subjunctive clause. Since it is found indifferently with, or without, a preceding subjunctive introduced by *ut*, the presence of the first subjunctive cannot be said to produce the second subjunctive, since the absence of the first does not prevent the occurrence of the second. Professors Zumpt and Madvig, along with their faithful followers, seem to have imagined that the one clause stands to the other in the relation of cause and effect, that the one clause precedes, and therefore produces, the other, is *post hoc*, and therefore *propter hoc*. This is a very common, but by no means correct, mode of reasoning.

A single chapter of Livy will supply what is sufficient for the application of this second argument.

Id vero laboris velut de integro initium fuit. nam nec explicare quicquam, nec statuere poterant: nec, *quod statutum esset*, manebat, omnia perscindente vento et rapiente.

But that was as it were the beginning of labour again. For neither could they spread out canvass, nor fasten poles: nor did, what had been fixed, remain fast, since the wind tore to pieces, or swept everything away. Lib. xxi. 58.

Here there is no preceding *ut* to account for the subjunctive statutum esset, which, besides being the same mood, is, moreover, the same tense as the now notorious—*quæ commentatus esset secum*. Of course, the real reason why the subjunctive is used, is because there is no single precise predication made with reference to a particular place or point of time, and the renewed effort without effect at different times to plant the poles, is exhibited with great force and beauty by means of the subjunctive—quod statutum esset.

This sentence has been taken as a specimen rather than a selection from many similar ones. The immediate context from which it is taken proves that the Roman writers wrote not at random, but by rule, and a rule which had its root in reason. In the very sentence before the one last quoted, Livy says— Tandem, effuso imbre, quum eo magis accensa vis venti esset, ipso illo, quo deprehensi erant, loco castra ponere necessarium visum est.

At length, the rain pouring down in torrents, when the fury of the wind had been all the more increased thereby, they were unavoidably compelled to pitch their camp on that very spot on which they had been overtaken by the storm.—Lib. xxi. 58.

Here in—deprehensi erant—there is the very same tense as in—statutum esset,—but because there is a predication made with all the definite precision of which language is capable—ipso illo—the indicative is used; whereas in—statutum esset—the predication being entirely indefinite, the subjunctive is used.

Nor is this all. The following sentence, resembling the one just quoted in the necessary particulars, is found at the close of the same chapter:—Multi homines, multa jumenta, elephanti quoque ex his, *qui* proelio ad Trebiam facto *superfuerant*, septem absumpti.

Here it will be observed that the predication is precise in all its particulars, and hence, as a matter of course, the pluperfect indicative is used.

III. A third proof that indefinite predication is peculiar to the pluperfect subjunctive, is found in the union of that tense with an indefinite particle itself.

Nec vis tantum militum movebat excitata præsentia ducis, sed quod Volscorum animis nihil terribilius erat quam ipsius Camilli forte oblata species: ita, *quocunque se intulisset*, victoriam secum haud dubiam trahebat.

Nor was it the impetuosity of the soldiers, fired by the presence of their leader, which produced such an effect, but because nothing was so alarming to the minds of the Volscians as the accidental appearance of Camillus himself: thus, to whatever place he had repaired, he drew certain victory in his train.—Livy, vi. 8.

In the same writer, in a chapter descriptive of the transit of the Alps, a passage is found with the same peculiarity in question.

Inde montani pauciores jam, et latrocinii magis quam belli more, concursabant; modo in primum, modo in novissimum agmen, utcunque aut locus opportunitatem daret, aut progressi morative aliquam occasionem fecissent.

Afterwards the mountaineers, by this time fewer in number, and more like freebooters than warriors, skirmished; at one time on the van, at another time on the rear, wherever either the ground offered a chance, or by marching ahead, or by lagging behind, they had made an opportunity for themselves.—Livy, xxi. 35.

Nothing can be clearer than the impossibility of rendering a predication more indefinite as to time and place, than by using the words modo—modo, and utcunque, with the pluperfect subjunctive.

It will have been seen from the numerous passages thus adduced, that this peculiar usage of the pluperfect subjunctive is found—

1*st.* With a preceding subjunctive clause.
2*d.* Without a preceding subjunctive clause.
3*d* With an indefinite particle.

There just was wanted one circumstance to crown and complete the proof of this usage of the subjunctive, to show that it was found in all conceivable cases, and that the two sentences last quoted have supplied in the word quicunque or a similar compound. The reviewer, however, who seems to have reached a foregone conclusion of his own, but will not perhaps be so successful in producing the conviction in others, that every doctrine of the author is false, condemns this doctrine of indefinite predication as a matter of course. And he labours hard to justify his prejudice. He taxes his industry, if not his invention, to adduce something or other, which may seem to dignify his opposition with the semblance, if not with the substance, of reason. But never was a result reached more directly the reverse of what was anticipated by its projector. The reviewer starts opinions, which, like wilful coursers with a weak charioteer, carry him to a terminus which he did not contemplate at the commencement of his career. He lifts weapons too heavy for him to wield, and instead of wounding his opponent, as he would wish, he only wounds himself.

He commences his assault with the most murderous intent, but he closes by committing self-destruction. The reviewer himself has "forgotten" that in the very column in which he has condemned the author for associating the idea of indefiniteness with the subjunctive, he has cited Dr Carson in defence of the same doctrine. "This *vagueness* or *indetermination* is in fact essential to the right application of the rule," putting Dr Carson's language in reference to this point in *italics*. Thus the same doctrine, in the judgment of the reviewer, is true or false according to the individual who, for the time being, holds it.

It would have been well for the reviewer if forgetfulness of the indefinites in question could have been with propriety and truth imputed to him. It is impossible for one who has never known a subject to forget it. Forgetfulness of a subject implies the possession of its previous knowledge. The reviewer, in imputing "forgetfulness of many indefinite clauses in Latin not placed in the subjunctive," has really conveyed a compliment, although he intended a censure. He resembles a certain personage in history, who, going out with the desire and design of cursing, was compelled to bless. Such is the gross inconsistency into which he has worked himself, who has undertaken the hopeless task of trying to make a rational theory irrational, and an irrational one rational.

The reviewer seems to imagine that the interpretation of the pluperfect subjunctive in the cases considered above is inconsistent with the fact that "quicunque and such indefinite words are generally joined with the indicative." There is not the slightest inconsistency in the two cases. The inconsistency is only in the imagination of the reviewer, or rather the wish was father of the thought, or, as old Cæsar puts it, Quod volunt homines, id plerumque credunt.

In the first place, those indefinite words with the indicative, to which the reviewer refers, generally have a different tense from what they have when joined with the subjunctive, and bear a different meaning. Quicunque, quicquid, in such combinations, are naturally equal to omnes, omnia. This is no mere arbitrary opinion, but a fact admitting of positive proof, a process which the reviewer habitually dispenses with, delighting in the more convenient process of assumption and assertion. In the following passage from Livy, omne is the actual antecedent of quicquid.

Itaque umbra vestri auxilii, Romani, tegi possumus; *quicquid* deinde habuerimus, *quicquid* ipsi fuerimus, vestrum *id omne* existimaturi.—Lib. vii. 30.

Such an expression as quæcunque feci, so common in Latin, is virtually equal to omnia quæ feci. It would be difficult to say whether quæcunque or such a combination with the indicative, or quocunque with the subjunctive—quocunque se intulisset—is more in accordance with the genius of the Latin language.

There is another argument—the last, but not the least—for these respective usages, which is furnished by the analogy of the Greek language. In the Anabasis of Xenophon the following passage occurs:—

'Οτου δι χιλος σταιιος ταχυ ειη, αυτος δ' εδυνατο παρασκευασασθαι δια το πολλους εχειν υπηρετας.—Lib. i. ix. 27.

Here the indefinite ὁτου with the Optative ειη is precisely parallel to Utcunque fecissent in the passage from Livy quoted above. Utcunque progressi mornative aliquam occasionem fecissent.

Again, in the same writer,—

Και στρατηγοι δε αυτοι απεδειξα ταυτων, ὁσοι εις Καστωλου πεδιον αθροιζονται.—Lib. i. 1, 2.

Here ὁσοι = quicunque, actually has as its antecedent ταυτων = Latin omnium, and of course is joined with the indicative αθροιζονται.

Such is the true usage of "quicunque, and those indefinite words which are generally joined with the indicative." It is left to others to determine whether the author really "*forgot*" their usage, or the reviewer ever *knew* their usage. The latter professes to entertain a profound horror of inconsistency. His only claim to consistency, however, is one—more curious than creditable — the consistency of inconsistency. He denounces the author's doctrine of an indefinite subjunctive, but he defends it in the case of Dr Carson. In this he sees nothing but consistency. He sees, however, great inconsistency between quicunque with the indicative and quicunque with the subjunctive. To use his own favourite imputation of forgetfulness, he has forgotten that there are casuists who strain at a gnat, but swallow a camel, just as there are mock moralists, who would weep pathetically over a dead donkey, but neglect their dying mother.

Thus far has the principle of indefinite predication been maintained against the "*essential*-part" theory, in explanation of incorporated subjunctive clauses. That theory has originated from an entire misconception of the true nature of the so-called "subjunctive" —of which much more will be said in due course. Few theories have either travelled so far, or been taken on trust by so many. It has travelled from Berlin to Copenhagen, from Copenhagen to London, from London to Edinburgh. The coin has long been current, but it is only counterfeit after all. It bears the name and superscription of the German Cæsar, the great lawgiver in philology, but it wants one thing, it bears not the genuine stamp of truth. Despite this drawback, however, the theory, in every country, by all classes of scholars, has been taken for granted, rather than taken on trial. As for the reviewer, indeed, it was not till once it had been assailed that he virtually abandoned it, but rather than adopt the principle of the author, he ventured to propound a new theory of his own. That theory the author does not deem it desirable to discuss, to pronounce any opinion on its truth or falsity, its value or its worthlessness. He has only to do with the reviewer indirectly, to deal with him as the partial defender of the German philological theorists. He has merely employed the article of the reviewer as a block on which to deal what he hopes will be the last blow to the essential-part theory. To show, however, that he is not at all jealous of this rival theory, he quotes it in full. "The clauses, from their close connexion with a reported thought or speech, have passed out of the form of direct statement into indirect, out of the definite into the indefinite."

This theory may be called the direct-indirect or the indirect-direct theory. Thus entitled, it is addressed to posterity. The author, however, will not warrant that it will reach its destination.

## CHAPTER II.

### GROTEFEND AND FORBIGER'S THEORY OF THE CONDITIONAL.

THE reviewer's idea of impossibility seems to be, the possibility of the author being right. What a moderately clear understanding would reject as absurd; what a moderately tender conscience would disclaim as unfair, that the reviewer, in his blind desire to damage conclusions he cannot disprove, adopts, without the slightest hesitation or compunction. Rather than admit that the author is right or that Grotefend is wrong, he seems prepared to admit or assert anything whatever. The reviewer broadly asserts "Mr Hamilton never seems to have caught the reasoning of Grotefend." There is a class of speakers and writers, who, dispensing with the process of proof, to compensate for the absence of argument, try to throw a double portion of strength into their assertions. The reviewer is a conspicuous representative of the aforesaid class. Assertion is clearly his forte. Since, however, his strong statements are usually, if not uniformly, incorrect, his strong point really becomes his weak point. The reviewer has made the strong statement quoted above, under the inspiration of his characteristic rashness, and, as might have been expected, with his usual fatal infelicity of result. The Nemesis of retribution is at his heels again.

Since the issue raised between the reviewer and the author is on the subject of the *Conditional*, the argument of the latter against the former may be stated appropriately in the conditional form. If, as the reviewer alleges, the author "has never caught the reasoning of Grotefend," then it follows that all the Universities of Scotland have been stricken with the same intellectual blindness. Professor Geddes, of the University of Aberdeen, to whom the subject was referred, in a document genuine and authentic, addressed to the author, states his opinion in the following manner:—" Regarding your assault on the canon of Grotefend relating to the subjunctive, I think decidedly you are victorious."

In the same way, Professor Sellar, lately of St Andrews University, states his opinion—" The canons which you impugn appear to me to be clearly wrong."

In the same way, Professor Ramsay, of the University of Glasgow, states his opinion—" There can be no doubt that Grotefend's rule on Si is altogether wrong, and that your principle is correct."

In the same way, Professor Blackie, of the University of Edinburgh, states his opinion—" I entirely agree with you as to Si."

Still to adhere to the conditional form of stating an argument, if the author is in error as to Si, he has good company to keep him in countenance. Indeed, he would rather be wrong with the Universities, than right with this anonymous scribe.

In the case of an imputation so purely personal as that now disposed of, however desirable it was for the author to cite the statements of others rather than his own, it was not at all necessary for the refutation of the reviewer. That unknown personage, with a facility fatal to himself, but fortunate for his opponent, forges the very weapons by which he falls in fight. Nothing more is needed than to continue the quotation of the reviewer himself, to show that the author "*has* caught the reasoning of Grotefend," and that his treatment of that German scholar is perfectly fair. "The first passage attacked is one to be found in the Rev. T. K. Arnold's Form of Grotefend's Materials for Translation into Latin. It runs thus—'Si, with the indicative, leaves the reality of the supposition entirely out of the question, conveying no intimation whatever of its possibility or impossibility, of its probability or improbability.' Then follow examples."

Why did the reviewer quote the rule of Grotefend, and omit his examples? If the reviewer had confidence in the correctness of Grotefend's rule, why did he not cite his examples in confirmation of it? And yet the reviewer is he who censured the author for "taking no notice of Zumpt's principle." What is to be thought of the consistency and sincerity of Satan reproving sin?

Quis tulerit Gracchos de seditione querentes!

In the reviewer's quotation it will be observed that Grotefend lays down as the result of his generalization a rule as to the usage of Si with the indicative, without any qualification or reserve whatever. Probably there never was a rule written whose application was less restricted by limitation or condition, although from the subject to which it relates the reverse might have been expected to be the case. Grotefend in its construction does not seem to have thought it required to be interpreted in connexion with its context. It would be a piece of gratuitous folly in his critic to adduce what Grotefend himself deemed unnecessary for the right understanding of his rule. The rule is complete in itself, though not correct. Here it is again, "Si with the indicative leaves the reality of the supposition entirely out of the question, conveying no intimation whatever of its possibility or impossibility, of its probability or improbability," and here is what Grotefend considered an exemplification of its truth, but what his champion the reviewer was afraid to quote. "*Si* fato omnia *fiunt*, nil nos admonere potest, ut cautiores simus." The reviewer, however, deems it essential to the argument of Grotefend to quote something else. He says, "Then Grotefend adds, 'It is only from the context that it can be determined whether the writer considered the supposition as a fact or real occurrence; but this is not implied by the indicative, this mood being used in cases when the writer certainly does *not* conceive the hypothesis to be of actual occurrence.'" He adds,

"Mr Hamilton does not quote the latter part of the last sentence, and its force seems to have escaped him, for he says that Grotefend assigns no reason for his rule."

After what has been seen above, it ill became the reviewer to impute partiality of quotation to the author. The principle on which he has proceeded throughout has not been to quote what conscience in fairness would have demanded for the author, but what his own convenience suggested. It is a pity he should have sacrificed so much, and yet gained so little. The allegation that "the force of the latter part of the sentence" in question "has escaped" the author, like all the rest of his allegations, admits of easy refutation. Grotefend's rule relative to *Si* is the result of an entire misconception of a peculiar usage of Si, of which the sentence—Si fato omnia fiunt, nihil nos admonere potest, ut cautiores simus—is a striking exemplification. This misconception is at once apparent, from what the reviewer considers to be a "reason of the rule," this mood, the indicative, according to Grotefend, quoted above, "being used in cases where the writer certainly does *not* conceive the hypothesis to be of actual occurrence." Of course, this is quite true, but that constitutes no justification of the rule of Grotefend. A Roman writer or speaker indeed uses the indicative with Si, "when he certainly does *not* consider the hypothesis to be of actual occurrence," but only to show that *the supposition itself is absurd from the consequences it entails*. This singularly effective method of reasoning was employed by the Greeks generally as well as by the Romans, and, as already pointed out by the author elsewhere, by Euclid in particular, under the name of *Reductio ad absurdum*. Grotefend failed to discover this, and gave to the world his erroneous generalization instead.

The reviewer, of course, rather than admit anything so odious to his mind, as that Grotefend should be wrong, or the author right, charges the latter at one time with misrepresentation, at another time with misconception, according as it suits, and proceeds to give what he supposes to be the fair and true meaning of the former. The author has much pleasure in quoting this new exposition of the reviewer. "Grotefend's reasoning is quite clear to our mind. One would naturally expect Si with the indicative to state a supposition which the writer believed to be a fact. But we are prevented from coming to this conclusion by finding it joined with the indicative in cases in which there is no doubt that the writer regarded the supposition as incredible. When *Si* therefore is joined with the indicative, we have to ascertain the writer's belief by some other means than the simple form of the words." To the first part of this exposition the author gives his ready assent—"One would naturally expect *Si* with the indicative to state a supposition which the writer believed to be a fact." His assent, however, goes no further. To the statement—"But we are prevented from coming to this conclusion by finding it joined with the indicative in cases in which there is no doubt that the writer regarded the supposition as incredible," he decidedly demurs. The fact that "Si is joined with the indicative in cases in which there is no doubt that the writer regarded the supposition as incredible," is no reason whatever why "we are prevented from coming to this conclusion," namely, "one would naturally expect *Si* with the indicative to state a supposition which the writer believed to be a fact." The reviewer seems to suppose that because Si is joined with the indicative in certain peculiar cases not very numerous, in which there is *a momentary assumption of the truth of what the writer knows to be false*, therefore Si is not joined at all with the indicative " to state a supposition which the writer believes to be a fact." This is a most monstrous conclusion, and quite opposed to the genius of the Latin language.

The reader will remember that Grotefend, as quoted above, has said, " it is only from the context that it can be determined whether the writer considered the supposition as a real fact." It is a common saying that there is no accounting for tastes. With as much truth it may be said there is no " accounting" for beliefs. By some idiosyncrasy or other Grotefend adopted a most improbable theory of the conditional. Of course, he was quite entitled to hold his own peculiar views on that subject. When, however, by publishing his theory on the subject, he sought to impose his belief on others, one would naturally have expected that he would have adduced more conclusive reasons in support of it. A theory before being accepted as true must approve itself to the common sense of men. Common sense requires that the propounder of a theory should exemplify it in practice. But Grotefend, who says that "it is only from the context that it can be determined whether the writer considered the supposition as a real fact," does not even give the reference to three separate passages, from each of which he extracts a sentence to illustrate his peculiar theory. Out of four sentences cited in imaginary confirmation of his rule, he gives reference to the context of one only. That sentence is to be found in Cicero, *Ros. Am.* 1, 53. An examination of that context will show that the only effect of the application of Grotefend's rule is to stultify Cicero and to mystify his readers.

Grotefend, in accordance with a practice too prevalent among his countrymen, a practice better adapted for speculation than demonstration, "has evolved the theory in question out of the depths of his own consciousness." Instead of calling into court the Roman writers, who are unquestionably the most competent witnesses as to the usage and laws of their own language, he has usurped the office of a witness, and has become at once witness, advocate, and judge in the present case. A court so constituted is not constituted according to the dictates of reason, and its decisions are not likely to be in accordance with the requirements of justice. Nor does the reviewer, in his method of arriving at a judgment, improve on the practice of Grotefend. Indeed, he is even inferior, for he does not cite the evidence of a single Latin writer, from the commencement of his article to its close. Either unable to find witnesses to corroborate his peculiar conclusions, or afraid that those he found from cross-examination might be made to turn against himself, for the evidence of others he has substituted his own assertions. The reviewer, confidently calculating that the credulity of others would be equal to his own, in the ecstasy of his temporary triumph forgot that there might be such a thing as a court of appeal, forgot the possibility of a new trial, a trial conducted according to the dictates of reason, and a decision consistent with the demands of equity.

The first witness that the author deems it desirable to summon in support of his opinion, and in opposition to the theory of Grotefend, is Virgil. No one who knows anything at all about the Latin language or Latin literature will venture to dispute that Virgil is a most competent and trustworthy witness. Flourishing in the very middle of the golden age of Latin literature, himself a scholar and consorting with scholars, the chosen companion and confidant of that brilliant group of men who graced the court of the Emperor Augustus, surely he, if any one at all, knew well the use and force of every Latin word. First, a passage will be extracted in illustration of Si with the indicative, and then another passage in illustration of Si with the subjunctive. And since Grotefend, as will be remembered, has said that "it is only from the context that it can be determined whether the writer considered the supposition as a fact or real occurrence," since, moreover, the reviewer, not satisfied with the author's exposition of Grotefend's meaning, has also said, " when Si, therefore, is joined with the indicative we have to ascertain the writer's belief by *some other means than the simple form of the word,*" the author, with every wish here, as in his former treatise, to give fair play to the propounder of the theory, and his champion, gives a very copious context in connexion with the use of Si with the indicative. The passage is a well known one, occurring in the *Æneid,* book vi. lines 509–534.

Ad quae haec Priamides: Nihil o tibi, amice! relictum.
Omnia Deiphobo solvisti, et funeris umbris.
Sed me fata mea et scelus exitiale Lacaenae
His mersere malis: illa haec monumenta reliquit.
Namque, ut supremam falsa inter gaudia noctem
Egerimus, nosti; et nimium meminisse necesse est.
Quum fatalis equus saltu super ardua venit
Pergama, et armatum peditem gravis attulit alvo;
Illa, chorum simulans, euantis orgia circum
Ducebat Phrygias: flammam media ipsa tenebat
Ingentem, et summa Danaos ex arce vocabat.
Tum me, confectum curis, somnoque gravatum,
Infelix habuit thalamus, pressitque jacentem
Dulcis et alta quies, placidaeque simillima morti.
Egregia interea conjunx arma omnia tectis
Emovet, et fidum capiti subduxerat ensem;

Intra tecta vocat Menelaum, et limina pandit:
Scilicet id magnum sperans fore munus amanti,
Et famam exstingui veterum sic posse malorum.
Quid moror? irrumpunt thalamo; comes additus una,
Hortator scelerum, Aeolides. Di, talia Graiis
*Instaurate, pio si poenas ore reposco.*
Sed, te qui vivum casus, age fare vicissim,
Attulerint. Pelagine venis erroribus actus?
An monitu divom? an quae te Fortuna fatigat,
Ut tristis sine sole domos, loca turbida, adires?
   Hac vice sermonum . . . . .

The entire speech of Deiphobus, the son of Priam, addressed to Æneas in the shades below, is here given, containing as it does the preceding and succeeding context of the sentence written in *italics*, selected to test the theory of Grotefend. With such a copious context, there can be no room for a charge of garbling Virgil with the desire and design of fixing a forced and far-fetched interpretation on one of his expressions detached from its immediate adjuncts. The author has had great pleasure in citing this copious context, and to all the advantages that may accrue from a consideration of it, he makes the defenders of Grotefend thoroughly welcome. They will have a full and fair opportunity of finding out the particular part of the context which "determines whether the supposition involved in 'Si reposco' is a fact or real occurrence." As for the reviewer, it is to be observed that in his paraphrase of the meaning of Grotefend, as

quoted above, he has abandoned that part of the
theory which requires the consideration of the context,
for his amendment is "when *Si* therefore is found
with the indicative, we have to ascertain the writer's
belief by some other means than the simple form of
the words." This is a very important and significant
change. If the reviewer abandoned the opinion that
a consideration of the "context" was essential to
"determine" whether the writer believed the supposition to be a real fact or occurrence, he was bound as
a *bona fide* expositor of the truth to specify in distinct
categorical terms what were the "means, when *Si* is
joined with the indicative, by which the writer's belief
is to be ascertained" apart from the "simple form of
the words." He has failed to do so, and the natural
presumption is, that he lacked the requisite ability.
And yet he has denied the truth of the author's principle. No man is justified in denying the doctrine
advocated by another, unless and until he is prepared
to prove that it is false, and to substitute a true one
in its place.

But it is high time to consider the two clauses which
constitute the sentence extracted above in *italics*, to
illustrate the true theory of Si when found with the
indicative—

Di, talia Graiis
Instaurate, pio si poenas ore reposco.

Do ye, O Gods, render the like to the Greeks, since
I breathe my prayer from patriotic lips.

Of course, the latter clause—pio si poenas ore

reposco—presents a very striking illustration of a purely rhetorical hypothesis. The nature of this peculiar usage of *Si* is explained and illustrated at great length by the author elsewhere. There is no need, therefore, here of a lengthened exposition of the usage. Suffice it to say, that the hypothesis introduced by Si in this and similar cases is not genuine or real, but only formal or rhetorical. The writer or speaker adopting this hypothetical form of expression, entertains not the slightest doubt whatever relative to what forms the subject of his thoughts. The conditional form of expression is chosen only that the conclusion contained in the consequent clause may be the more readily conceded. And so here, the rhetorical hypothesis—pio si poenas ore reposco—contains the very plea on which the prayer—Di, talia Graiis instaurate—is preferred by a patriotic Trojan against the cruel Greeks. This rhetorical hypothesis has never yet been seen by the author in connexion with the subjunctive,—a fact of itself fatal to the theory of Grotefend, though there were no other to urge against it. But there is no need of pressing a negative proof into the service here. Let the theory, like a tree, be tested by its fruit. Let the theory be applied to the passage under consideration. If, according to Grotefend, "*Si* leaves the reality of the supposition entirely out of the question, conveying no intimation whatever of its possibility or impossibility, of its probability or improbability," or, according to the reviewer, the writer's or speaker's " belief," when Si is joined with the indicative, cannot thereby be ascertained, Deiphobus, in preferring an earnest request to the gods, "conveyed no intimation whatever or belief in the probability of his own plea." How, in the name of common sense, could the gods be expected to hear the prayer of a man who did not believe in the reality of the plea urged in behalf of it? Sincerity in entertaining beliefs, and earnestness in the expression of them, have been the characteristics of honest suppliants, whether in ancient or modern times. If, however, the theory of Grotefend be true, and the defence of his champion, the reviewer, be valid, this common opinion would appear not to be correct.

Next, let the truth of the theory when applied to the subjunctive be tested. The theory as applicable, first to the indicative, and then to the subjunctive, is thus fully stated in the words of Grotefend:—"A supposition may be so stated as either to imply nothing with respect to the speaker's opinion, or, on the other hand, to convey with it some intimation that it is in his judgment possible, probable, etc. When Si carries with it no such intimation, it governs the indicative; *when it does carry any intimation of the kind, it governs the subjunctive.*" The latter part of the theory, which now falls to be considered, has been put in *italics*. The first circumstance that will strike an observant student of the Latin language is the entire absence of a principle on which to found the theory. The theory is distinguished, not for its strict consistency, but for its uniform capriciousness. If a con-

sideration of the "context" be necessary for the right
understanding of *Si* when joined with the indicative,
why is a consideration of the "context" not necessary
for a right understanding of Si when joined with the
subjunctive? If, in the case of the indicative, according to the reviewer, "we have to ascertain the writer's
belief by some other means than the simple form of
the words," why is it not so in the case of the subjunctive? Nor is this all. The theory is contrary to the
entire analogy of the Latin language. One of the
most striking characteristics of the Latin language is
the employment of the subjunctive in quoting statements or sentiments which are *not the writer's own*.
When a Latin writer wishes to mark an opinion for
which he is not responsible, and accordingly repudiates, he employs the subjunctive. And yet
Grotefend, in opposition to this universally recognised
practice, says, "When a supposition is so stated as to
convey with it some intimation that it is in his judgment possible, probable, etc., it governs the subjunctive." In like manner, when a writer or speaker
wishes to intimate that the opinion expressed by him
is his own, that he is responsible for it, and that he
believes it to be true, he employs the indicative.
And yet Grotefend says, "A supposition may be so
stated as to imply nothing with respect to the speaker's
opinion. When *Si* carries with it no such intimation,
it governs the indicative." The indicative and subjunctive do not lose their peculiar characteristics when
joined with Si or any other particle whatever, but

## THEORY OF THE CONDITIONAL. 45

retain them with the most uniform consistency. The only effect, however, of the theory of Grotefend is to pervert and confound the characteristics peculiar to the indicative and subjunctive. This conclusion, apparent when the theory is tried by the general analogy of the Latin language, as indicated above, will be still more apparent when it is tried by the following illustrative example, taken also, as in the previous case, from Virgil, *Æn.* vi. 625.

> Non, mihi *si* linguae centum *sint*, oraque centum,
> Ferrea vox, omnes scelerum comprendere formas,
> Omnia poenarum percurrere nomina, possim.

The clause in this substance which either accredits or discredits the theory is—Mihi si linguæ centum sint. According to it, "when *Si* conveys some intimation that the supposition is in the judgment of the speaker possible, probable, etc., it governs the subjunctive." Here *Si* governs the subjunctive. Hence the speaker, the priestess of Apollo, "conveyed the intimation that she might probably have a hundred tongues." This complement of the theory relative to the subjunctive, which imputes to a woman the possibility or probability of having a hundred tongues, is in every way worthy of the other complement relative to the indicative, which imputes to a man the probability of preferring a prayer to the gods without expressing his belief in the reality of the plea he urges,—

> Par nobile fratrum!

Such is the theory of Grotefend. As an *a priori* conception, it is directly opposed to the entire analogy of the Latin language. What is peculiar to the indicative it imputes to the subjunctive; what is peculiar to the subjunctive it imputes to the indicative. Its tendency is thus to pervert the laws that regulate the construction of Latin speech. Instead of inaugurating the principle of logical consistency, it introduces the operation of lawless caprice. It was the result, undoubtedly, on the part of Grotefend, of a one-sided and rash generalization, but it is only charity to believe that had he lived longer, he would himself have detected and corrected his own mistakes.

It is certainly very curious that the only form of a hypothetical proposition in the Latin language which with any show of plausibility could be so interpreted as to seem to give countenance to the theory of Grotefend has escaped his observation, and never been discovered by any of his defenders. A fatal inconsistency and a fatal infelicity has followed the theory throughout. The passages which have been quoted in favour of it have been proved to be fatal to it; and those passages which, with some plausibility at least, might seem to favour it, have been forgotten. Such a passage is the following, which, like the two preceding ones, is taken from Virgil,—

> Contemplator item, quum se nux plurima sylvis
> Induet in florem, et ramos curvabit olentes :

*Si superant* foetus, pariter frumenta sequentur,
Magnaque cum magno veniet tritura calore :
At, *si* luxuriâ foliorum *exuberat* umbra,
Nequidquam pingues paleâ teret area culmos.
— *Geor.* lib. i. 187.

Here are two suppositions introduced by Si with the indicative—*si superant*—*si exuberat*. There is nothing whatever to intimate directly, or to indicate indirectly, which supposition Virgil believes to be a fact. As for the context, whatever Grotefend may say, it can throw no light whatever on the subject, for the sentence which precedes the extract, and the sentence which succeeds it, bears no relation to it. The sentence which precedes the extract is—

Saepe exiguus mus
Sub terris posuitque domos atque horrea fecit;
Aut, oculis capti, fodere cubilia talpae;
Inventusque cavis bufo, et quae plurima terrae
Monstra ferunt: populatque ingentem farris acervum
Curculio, atque inopi metuens formica senectae.

The sentence which succeeds the extract is—

Semina vidi equidem multos medicare serentes,
Et nitro prius et nigra perfundere amurca;
Grandior ut foetus siliquis fallacibus esset.

Virgil thus conveying no intimation whatever, either directly or indirectly, as to which of the two suppositions—si superant foetus,—si exuberat umbra,

—he believed to be a fact, and the context conveying, if possible, still less; it might be maintained with some plausibility, at least in this form of a hypothetical proposition, that " Si with the indicative leaves the reality of the supposition entirely out of the question, conveying no intimation whatever of its possibility or impossibility, of its probability or improbability." But the inference even in this case would not be correct. Virgil, indeed, does not intimate which supposition is the more probable, but he implies that either is very probable, and this alone justifies the use of the indicative. The one supposition is not inconsistent with the other. In one year there might be an abundance of fruit, when *si superant foetus* could be a fact; while, on the other hand, si exuberat umbra, could be a mere supposition. In another year there might be a superabundance of leaves, when si luxuria foliorum exuberat umbra would be a fact; while, on the other hand, *si superant foetus* could be a mere supposition. The supposition in either case is very probable; in one year or another, it is a fact. This is a sufficient explanation and justification of the indicative.

The theory of a double hypothesis may be stated thus:—A writer, when, in introducing a double hypothesis, by giving the preference to neither, he seems to express no opinion at all, really implies by the indicative the great probability of either, neither being inconsistent with the other. That this is the case is proved conclusively and decisively by the two following passages taken from Livy:—

Coepere a fame mala, *sive* adversus annus frugibus *fuit, sive* dulcedine concionum et urbis deserto agrorum cultu: *nam utrumque traditur.*

These misfortunes commenced with a famine, whether because the year was not favourable for the fruits of the earth, or because the tillage of the fields was abandoned from a love for public meetings and the city; for both traditions exist.—Lib. iv. 12.

Empulum eo anno ex Tiburtibus haud memorando certamine captum: *sive* duorum consulum auspicio bellum ibi gestum *est, ut scripsere quidam: sive* per idem tempus Tarquiniensium quoque *sunt* vastati agri a Sulpicio consule, quo Valerius adversus Tiburtes legiones duxit.

In that year Empulum was taken from the Tiburtines in an engagement by no means noteworthy: whether the war was carried on there under the auspices of the two consuls, as some historians have written: or the territories of the inhabitants of Tarquinii were also laid waste about the same time that Valerius led his legions against the Tiburtines.—Lib. vii. 18.

The reviewer, as has already been remarked, failed to state how a writer's belief was to be ascertained, "when employing Si with the indicative." He, however, has done as good service, though contrary to his desire and design, by stating how it was *not* to be ascertained. From the specimens given of his arguments, that is, his assertions, this rule may very fairly be generalized; whatever he lays down may be regarded as the reverse of right. Therefore, since he said, "When Si is joined with the indicative, we have to ascertain the writer's belief by some other means than the simple form of the words," it may safely be inferred that the writer's belief *is* ascertained by the simple form of the words. The reviewer himself could have seen this, had he asked the meaning of the term *mood*. A school-boy of ordinary ability and attainment would have answered that—it is the mode of stating a proposition. According to the nature of the proposition, and the mode in which he wishes to present it, a Latin writer employs the indicative or subjunctive mood. Very often, in Latin, the only difference between a proposition when expressed by the indicative mood, and when expressed by the subjunctive mood, is a difference of form—a difference which is expressed by the termination of the verb, without imposing on the readers the necessity of turning back to consider the context. By no other means than the mechanism of moods could this difference of form have been expressed. Each mood when joined with a particle retains the same characteristic peculiarity that it does when it stands alone. This holds good in the case of ut, quum, dum, etc., when joined with the indicative and when joined with the subjunctive; and, as might have been expected, it holds good in the case of Si with the indicative and subjunctive. When the Latins wished to express that the reality was the reverse of the conception, they did so by the mere form of the word—the subjunctive, *e. g.*—utinam saperes, *i.e.* you are not wise, but I wish you were. Si fecisses aliter, te laudassem, *i.e.* you have not done so, but if you had, I would have praised thee. On the other hand, as might have been expected, when the Latins wished to express that the reality and the conception coincided, or were likely to do so, they did so by the mere form of the word,—the indicative mood, *e.g.* Si quid virtus et ingenium valent, ad ultimum vinces.

The following additional examples from very various Latin writers are cited to confirm these principles in opposition to the theory of Grotefend,—Equites enim vocabantur primi: octoginta inde primae classis centuriae: ibi *si variaret, quod raro incidebat*, ut secundae classis vocarentur.—Livy, i. 43. Had Grotefend seen the words marked in italics, he never would have written "When Si conveys some intimation with it that the supposition is in the writer's judgment probable, it governs the subjunctive."

Atqui, *si* nox opportuna *est* eruptioni, *sicut est*, haec profecto noctis aptissima hora est.—Livy, lib. vii. 35.

*Si* tamen interea quid in his ego perditus oris,
　　Quod te *credibile est* quaerere, *quaeris*, agam.
　　　　　　　　　　　　—Ovid, *Tr.* 3, 5, 23.

Quod *si, ut suspicor*, hoc novum ac repertum
　　Munus *dat* tibi Sulla litterator, etc.
　　　　　　　　　　　　—Catullus, xiv. 8.

Had Grotefend ever seen the clauses marked in *italics* in these sentences, he never would have written—"Si with the indicative leaves the reality of the supposition entirely out of the question, conveying no intimation whatever of its probability or improbability." The additional explanatory clause conveying assurance or probability, of which these instances have just been given, only are found with the indicative, not with the subjunctive, and never would have been employed by the Latins if they had meant that the assurance or probability was to be gathered from the "context."

But Grotefend is not the only one among eminent German scholars that has entertained and published opinions relative to the functions of Si at once erroneous and defective. The opinions of Albertus Forbiger are equally remarkable in this respect, and the greater celebrity of his name has caused a correspondingly wider circulation of his errors in this country. The following is a transcript of a translation of his commentary on a certain well-known passage in Virgil :—

> Di tibi *si* qua pios respectant numina, si quid
> Usquam justitia *est* et mens sibi conscia recti,
> Praemia digna ferant.—*Æneid,* lib. i. 603.

"The other reading, *justitiae,* would mean, ' If there is any justice on earth,' a doubt which would ill come from Æneas at the time when he had a most distinct evidence of its existence."

The common reading may be the correct reading, but certainly not for the reason here assigned, since it conveys as much doubt as the one here rejected; that is, none at all. The supposition introduced by

*Si* in the line quoted above is hypothetical only in form. It excludes doubt with all the force of which emphasis is capable, by invoking the almost universal and unanimous belief of mankind in the existence of a divinity which recognises and rewards what is right, and by appealing to the testimony of conscience, echo of the voice of God within the breast of man. Of course, the clause—*Si* quid usquam justitia *est*—contains a most clear and conspicuous illustration of the formal or rhetorical use of Si, and the faultless fidelity with which Grotefend's translator has performed the part of a copying clerk, instead of exercising the judgment of an independent thinker, presents an equally clear and conspicuous illustration of the too common credulity with which German criticism has been received in this country. Of the formal or rhetorical use of *Si*, Forbiger was as far from forming any conception as even his translator, and the only effect which his interpretation of Si can have is, like that of Grotefend, to stultify the classics and to mystify their readers.

The last criticism of the reviewer now falls to be disposed of, and the last notice to be taken of himself. Speaking of the author, he says, "If he had been in the habit of reading the works of the most scholarly of the Germans, he would have found Forbiger treated with the utmost contempt." In the reviewer's eager haste to impugn the author's "reading," it has never occurred to him that his own reasoning is completely at fault. The author is quite ready to admit with the reviewer that Forbiger has been reviled by certain of his own countrymen. That fact, however, so far from being injurious to the repute of Forbiger, will be regarded by all who can reason rightly as at once the penalty and proof of his fame. The practice of certain individuals, not the most charitable or competent of the human race, to revile those whom they cannot rival, is a practice common to all countries, and not confined to Germany alone. If the reviewer had reasoned more he would have known this, and he would have remarked less on the author's "reading." He could thus have proved himself to have been an abler logician and a better man. Forbiger's real reputation in his own country may be inferred from his reputation in this country. Here his reputation is truly great. Several years ago, Professor Ramsay, of the University of Glasgow, anxious to put the most correct text of Lucretius into the hands of his students, determined to select as his chief guide the edition of Forbiger. A few years later, the publishers to the University of Glasgow agreed to select Forbiger as their authority when attempting to secure a correct text of Virgil, designed for Scottish schools. That edition contains the commentary of Forbiger on the passage in Virgil last explained. In that commentary he has given full effect to his peculiar theory of the conditional. Seeing that the effect of his errors would be proportionate to the extent of his authority and influence, the greater necessity existed for detecting and correcting them.

It is only with the reviewer, of course, in the capacity of champion of Carson, Forbiger, Grotefend, and Zumpt, that the author has anything to do. He has gladly and gratefully availed himself of the opportunity offered to him of defending his opinions as originally given to the world, in opposition to these distinguished scholars. To the reviewer, however, no thanks are due. In parting with him, the author only has to state that he entertains little respect for his scholarship or critical faculty, still less for his ability as a logician, and least of all for his honour as a man. No great scholar could have written the article in question; no good man would have written it. No brave or good man would write under the cover of anonymous authorship that to which he would be afraid or ashamed to append his signature. The author feels persuaded that the author of this anonymous article would have both been ashamed and afraid to have acknowledged it by adhibiting his name; for it could not have failed to have damaged him, both personally and professionally. At the commencement of his article, he spoke of a certain book as a school-book. There is another school-book, to whose spirit, from the commencement to the close of his article, he has constantly run counter; while oftener than once in the course of his exposition he has been guilty of the grave offence forbidden in its stern command—*" Thou shalt not bear false witness against thy neighbour."*

# CHAPTER III.

### THE THEORY OF "DEPENDENCE."

THE propounders of those theories which have been subjected to the scrutiny of examination in the preceding chapters, and some others which remain to be subjected to a similar ordeal, seem to have laboured under the impression that it was the function of grammar to give laws to language, whereas it is the function of language to give laws to grammar. The Latin language will do this when it is allowed to become its own interpreter. To its careful student, who proceeds on the inductive principle of collecting and comparing facts and phenomena, it will suggest the laws by which it is governed. The primary and paramount principle which the Latin language suggests—as deducible from its writers in the Augustan age—on which its construction is based, is—that the syntax requires to be subordinate to the sense. In plainer language, this is neither more nor less than the principle of common sense. On the other hand, the theories which have been examined, and those which still remain to be examined, require, as the first condition of their application, that the sense must be sacrificed without scruple to the syntax. Such theories are equally irreconcilable with the genius of the Latin language, and the actual facts and phenomena which it presents. Just as in politics the safety of the state is the first and highest consideration, the supreme law, to which all others give way, so in Latin philology the sense of a sentence is the first and highest consideration, the supreme law, for which the ordinary conventional rules are suspended when it requires to make the demand. The following are clear and conspicuous instances of this practice:—

I. There is a Latin rule, common to all grammars, which says—" Substantives signifying the same thing agree in case." A Latin writer, however, would not say, Vixi Romae, urbis Italiae, but Vixi Romae, in urbe Italiae.

II. There is a Latin rule common to all grammars, which says—" Conjunctions couple like cases and moods." Virgil, however, says—

Dic, . . . et eris mihi magnus Apollo.

A still more remarkable instance of the suspension of this common rule is furnished by the following sentence from Livy:—

Canuleios igitur Iciliosque consules fore. Ne id Jupiter Optimus maximus sineret, regiae majestatis imperium eo recidere; et se *morituros quam* ut tantum dedecoris *patiantur*.—Lib. iv. 2.

It will be observed that the common rule would require passuros after *morituros quam*. This sentence throws great light on the true theory of the subjunctive, and will be quoted again for that purpose at a subsequent stage of this treatise.

III. There is a Latin rule, common to all grammars, which says—" Direct, independent questions require the indicative." Juvenal, however, says—

Quis tulerit Gracchos de seditione querentes.

This question is quite direct and independent, and yet the subjunctive, not the indicative, is used. The sentence, like the one preceding, is altogether remarkable, and will again be referred to. It is exactly parallel to the following one from Virgil:—

Quis possit fallere amantem?—*Æn*. iv. 296.

These principles, with the illustrations pertinent to them, have been laid down here before introducing the doctrine of "dependence." They show that when any change takes place in the ordinary constructions of Latin syntax, the change arises not from caprice, but from causes perfectly consistent with its exquisitely logical character, and always has the effect of making the syntax subordinate to the sense. The doctrine of dependence, on the other hand, whether or no there be anything in a dependent clause to justify the subjunctive at all, is disfigured in the first place by gross and glaring inconsistencies. It has just been seen that independent clauses are found with the subjunctive, in opposition to the rule of grammarians, but in perfect consistency with the genius of the Latin language; and the following sentences will show dependent clauses with the indicative, in opposition to the grammarians, but in perfect harmony with the grammar,—

> Viden' *ut* geminae *stant* vertice cristae,
> Et pater ipse suo superum jam *signat* honore?
> —Vir. *Æn.* vi. 780.
> 
> Adspice, *ut* insignis spoliis Marcellus opimis
> *Ingreditur*, victorque viros supereminet omnis!
> *Id.* 856.

A dependent clause being thus found with the indicative as well as with the subjunctive, and an independent clause being found with the subjunctive as well as the indicative, it follows that "dependence," as it is called, is a mere accident so far as either the subjunctive or indicative is concerned. The presence of "dependence" cannot produce the subjunctive, because its absence cannot prevent the occurrence of the subjunctive. The subjunctive is entirely independent of "dependence," and the indicative is not dependent on "independence." If "dependence" were the true essential cause of the subjunctive, it would be uniformly found with the subjunctive, and independence, in like manner, would be uniformly found with the indicative. But if even this were the case, what affinity is there between "dependence" and reported speech, which requires the subjunctive? There is not a whit more affinity between the one and the other, than there is between the angle of polarization and either. The laws that regulate the construction of the Latin language are uniform and consistent; the theories that are devised to explain these laws ought to be uniform and consistent likewise.

Dependence may be defined as a peculiar combination of words, which, as some grammarian or other once conceived, and others hitherto have believed, requires of itself the subjunctive. There is no virtue or reason in the combination itself which requires the subjunctive. This is proved by the fact, that the form of dependence,—*e.g.* a verb and particle followed by another verb,—at one time takes the indicative, at another time takes the subjunctive. What, of course, determines the mood in each particular instance is the sense to which, as has been shown by the practice of the Latins, all conventional rules give place. According to the rule of "dependence," *Aspice ut* would require the subjunctive ingrediatur. Virgil, however, as quoted above, has written ingreditur. On the other hand, Livy, when the sense required the subjunctive, in accordance with the genius of the Latin language, wrote—

Extemplo advocato concilio, scelera in se fratris, originem nepotum, *ut* geniti, *ut* educati, *ut cogniti essent*, caedem deinceps tyranni, seque ejus auctorem ostendit.—Lib. i. 6.

The following usages, which conventionally would

be called instances of "dependence," are really and clearly related to reported speech, which a writer employs when he wishes to state what is *not known* to him personally,—

Terrorem repente ex somno excitatis subita res et nocturnus pavor praebuit; ad hoc multorum *inscitia, qui, aut unde, hostes advenissent.*—Livy, vii. 12.

Cujus populi ea, cujusque gentis classis *fuerit, nihil certi est.*—Livy, vii. 26.

Hic L. Tarquinius (Prisci Tarquinii regis filius neposne *fuerit, parum liquet:* pluribus tamen auctoribus filium ediderim) fratrem habuerat Aruntem Tarquinium, mitis ingenii juvenem.—Livy, i. 46.

Ibi cum, *inscia multitudine quid ageretur,* proelia parva inter Romam Gabiosque fierent, quibus plerumque Gabina res superior esset; tum certatim summi infimique Gabinorum Sex. Tarquinium dono Deûm sibi missum ducem credere.—Livy, i. 54.

*Nescis quo valeat* nummus? *quem praebeat* usum?
—Hor. Sat. i. lib. i. 73.

To the same category as ignorance belong verbs of forgetting, wondering, inquiry, doubting, hazarding, disputing, deliberating, all of which, bearing a common reference to what is *not known or not certain,* independent of "dependence," are fitly used with the subjunctive.

Sed silentium triste ac tacita moestitia ita defixit omnium animos, ut prae metu *obliti, quid relinquerent, quid secum ferrent,* deficiente consilio, rogitantesque alii alios, nunc in liminibus starent, nunc errabundi domos suas, ultimum illud visuri, pervagarentur.—Livy, i. 29.

Tarquinium moribundum cum, qui circa erant, excepissent, illos fugientes lictores comprehendunt: clamor inde concursusque populi, *Mirantium quid rei esset.*—Livy, i. 41.

Et libri *aditi* (the Sibylline books were consulted by repairing to them) quinam finis aut remedium ejus mali ab diis *daretur.*—Livy, x. 47.

A plerisque *rogitantibus* dimissi, "Ecquod feminis quoque asylum *aperuissent ?* "—Livy, i. 9.

Ad ea elicienda ex mentibus divinis, Jovi Elicio aram in Aventino dicavit, Deumque *consuluit* auguriis, quae suscipienda *essent.*—Livy, i. 20.

Quid tandem est, cur coelum ac terras *misceant ?*—Livy, iv. 3.

Cum pavidus ille, quid *vellet*, quaereret; Serviliusque "causam dicendam esse," proponeret "crimenque, a Minucio delatum ad senatum, diluendum:" tunc Maelius recipere se in catervam suorum.—Livy, iv. 14.

*Incertos* quid *ageret,* nox oppressit.—Livy, vii. 34.

Non caedes, non fuga alterius partis, sed nox *incertos*, victi victoresne *essent* diremit.—Livy, ix. 23. The expression in this sentence is almost identical with that of the preceding one.

Profecti legati ad Fabium quum senatus consultum tradidissent, adjecissentque orationem convenientem mandatis, consul, demissis in terram oculis, tacitus ab *incertis*, quidnam *esset* acturus, legatis recessit.—Livy, ix. 38.

Non *incertis*, qua data victoria *esset*, intervenit: lux insequens victorem victumque ostendit.—Livy, x. 12.

Nec tamen ab dictatore comitia sunt habita, quia, vitione *creatus esset, in disquitionem venit.*—Livy, viii. 23.

Quod ubi ad aures accidit regis: adjecit extemplo animum satis suis substititque *dubius an transiret.*—Livy, viii. 24.

Vicit disciplina militaris, vicit imperii majestas, quae *in discrimine* fuerint, an ulla post hanc diem *essent.*—Livy, viii. 34.

Id *ambigitur*, bellinc gerendi causa *creatus sit;* an ut *esset*, qui ludis Romanis, quia L. Plautius praetor gravi morbo forte implicitus erat, signum mittendis quadrigis daret.—Livy, viii. 40.

Fabius consul, terrore urbi quoque injecto, stationem ante portas agebat: cum equites, procul visi, non sine terrore ab dubiis, quinam *essent*, mox cogniti, tantam ex metu laetitiam fecere, ut clamor urbem pervaderet.—Livy, iv. 40.

*Controversia* (dispute) inde fuit utrum populi jussu *indiceretur* bellum, *an satis esset* senatus consultum.—Livy, iv. 30.

Haud dubium fuit, quin Lucerinis opem Romanus ferret, bonis ac fidelibus sociis: simul ne Apulia omnis ad praesentem terrorum deficeret: ea modo, qua *irent consultatio fuit.*—Livy, ix. 2.

Aliquam diu utrimque intenti steterunt *expectantes* ut ab adversariis clamor et pugna *inciperet.*—Livy, ix. 32.

## THE THEORY OF "DEPENDENCE."

Tarquinii, ut Sextus, qui Romae relictus fuerat, ignarus responsi expersque imperii esset, rem summa ope taceri jubent; ipsi inter se, *uter prior*, cum Romam redissent, matri osculum *daret*, sorti permittunt.—Livy, i. 56.

There is another class of verbs, different indeed from those illustrated above, but not diverse, and still more closely and clearly connected with reported speech, in the following usage with the subjunctive. Of course this subjunctive is entirely independent of "dependence."

Tum legatis Tullus *dicendi* potestatem, quid petentes *venerint*, facit.—Livy, i. 22.

Ex eo ira regi mota; eludensque artem, ut ferunt, "Agedum," inquit, divine tu, *inaugura*, fierine *possit*, quod nunc ego mente concipio.—Livy, i. 36.

Quo coacto, per quot annos pro libertate *dimicent* cum Romanis, *exponunt.*—Livy, x. 16.

Vixdum satis armis aptatis, in ordines eunt: et clamore magis quam oculis hostem noscunt: nec, *quantus numerus sit*, æstimari potest.—Livy, x. 33.

Itaque huic indici *quid* fieri *vellent praeceperunt.*—Cor. Nepos, *Paus.* iv. 4.

> Extemplo socios, primumque arcessit Acesten;
> Et Jovis imperium, et cari praecepta parentis,
> *Edocet*, et quae nunc animo sententia *constet.*
> Vir. *Æn.*, v. 746.

But however clear it may appear that the cognate class of verbs now illustrated should require the subjunctive, from their peculiar signification, apart altogether from any virtue whatever supposed to be inherent in that combination of words conventionally called "dependence," it will probably at once occur to many, that there is one verb, *scire*, the very opposite of verbs of ignorance, doubting, deliberating, disputing, &c., which, no less uniformly than these, is followed by the subjunctive. However formidable at first sight this objection may appear, however hard it may seem to reconcile two usages so diametrically opposed, it will be found in this, as in every other case, that the law by which the Latin language is regulated is consistency but not caprice. Although *scire* and *nescire* stand to each other as day and darkness, the usage of each with the subjunctive is consistent with the true theory of that mood. The first passage, selected as a specimen of a verb of knowing joined with the subjunctive, is taken from Virgil:—

> Ergo his aligerum dictis affatur Amorem:
> Nate, meae vires, mea magna potentia; solus,
> Nate, patris summi qui tela Typhoia temnis;
> Ad te confugio, et supplex tua numina posco.
> Frater ut Aeneas pelago tuus omnia circum
> Littora *jactetur*, odiis Junonis iniquae,
> *Nota tibi*: et nostro doluisti saepe dolore.

Therefore, she (Venus) addresses the winged god of love in these words: My son, my strength, my great defence; thou alone art proof against the darts hurled on the giants by Jove supreme; to thee I repair, and as a suppliant invoke thine aid. It is well known to thee how thy brother Aeneas is tempest-tossed on every shore, by reason of the hate of jealous Juno: and thou hast often sympathized with our sorrows.— *Æn.* i. 663.

Here, in *nota tibi ut jactetur*, what is known as a fact, contrary to what might have been expected, is expressed by the subjunctive. The apparent anomaly, however, is accounted for when there is an exception or limitation made to the extent of the thing known. It will be observed that the emphatic word in the passage throughout is *tu*,—*tuus Aeneas*,—*nota tibi*, *nostro doluisti dolore*. The thing known was not known to the whole world. It was Cupid that had sympathized with the sorrow of Venus. Such seems to be the interpretation of the passage. Of course, it is quite possible, nay, even probable, that one such passage might be found containing a number of clauses so constructed as to favour the interpretation thus given, and yet not furnish a basis broad enough on which to build a general conclusion. But this is no solitary passage. There are many other similar ones in Virgil. The following additional one, which resembles the first in several respects, may be adduced in confirmation,—

At Venus interea Neptunum, exercita curis,
Alloquitur, talisque effundit pectore questus:
Junonis gravis ira nec exsaturabile pectus

Cogunt me, Neptune, preces descendere in omnis:
Quam nec longa dies, pietas nec mitigat ulla;
Nec Jovis imperio fatisve infracta quiescit.
Non media de gente Phrygum exedisse nefandis
Urbem odiis satis est, nec poenam traxe per omnem
Reliquias: Trojae cineres atque ossa peremptae
Insequitur. Caussas tanti sciat illa furoris.
Ipse mihi, nuper Lybicis, *tu testis*, in undis
Quam molem subito *excierit*.

But in the meantime Venus, harassed with care, addresses Neptune, and from her inmost breast pours forth this plaint: The deadly wrath and implacable hostility of Juno, whom neither length of time nor any pious deed can lull, and who, not even curbed by Jove and Fate's command, desists, compel me, O God of Ocean, to have recourse to every form of prayer. It is not enough for her accursed hate to have blotted out a city from the midst of Phrygian tribes, and to have dragged its remnant through every kind of woe: she pursues with vengeance the very ashes and bones of Troy in ruins. Let her know what is the cause of such resentment. You yourself, lately in the Libyan waters, were the witness with me of what a storm she raised.—*Æn.* v. 779.

Here, besides Venus herself, the power or opportunity of witnessing what took place was limited to Neptune (tu testis). This principle of limitation receives still further confirmation from the following passage in Nepos,—

Hic in navem, omnibus ignotus nautis, ascendit; quae cum tempestate maxima Naxum ferretur, ubi tum Atheniensium erat exercitus, sensit Themistocles, si eo pervenisset, sibi esse pereundum. Hac necessitate coactus domino navis *quis sit aperit*, multa pollicens si se conservasset.

Here a stranger to all the sailors, he went on board a ship, and when it in a heavy gale was drifting on Naxos, Themistocles saw that if he landed there he must die. Compelled by this exigency, he discloses to the master of the ship who he is, making many promises, if he would save his life.—*Them.* viii. 6.

This passage is very significant. He *only* tells his secret to the *captain*: he preserves his incognito to the crew.

The following passage from Livy combines the same condition and points to the same conclusion. The usage is not confined to one Latin custom but common to all.

Et, "ut re ipsa," inquit, "sciatis Quirites, quam *mihi* diuturna non *placeant* imperia, dictatura me abdico."

And that you may know, Romans, quoth he, how displeasing an extended period of command is to me, by the act itself, I lay down the office of dictator.—Lib. iv. 24.

Here again the pronoun is emphatic. It was Aemilius *only* that did not like a lengthened term of office. His countrymen generally were troubled by o such scruples.

## THE THEORY OF "DEPENDENCE." 69

But this principle of limitation is not by any means restricted to persons. It applies to time as well. The well-known expression in Virgil is an illustration,—

> Nunc scio quid sit amor.

The subjunctive *sit* implies that a feeling now is understood which was not understood before.

This change in a feeling is not only implied but expressly declared in the following passage, also taken from Virgil,—

> Hunc Polydorum, auri, quondam, cum pondere magno,
> Infelix priamus furtim mandarat alendum
> Threicio regi; quum *jam diffideret* armis
> Dardaniae, cingique urbem obsidione videret.
> *Æn.* iii. 49.

Here the *jam* in quum jam diffideret, as the *nunc* in the preceding *nunc scio quid sit*, expresses a feeling which did not exist before. The form of expression does not bear the remotest resemblance to "dependence," and yet the subjunctive has the same peculiar force as clauses that are called dependent; so that it is quite clear that the mood is entirely independent of "dependence." In the following sentence from Livy, there is the very identical form of expression, with of course the same meaning, as in the sentence just quoted from Virgil.

Lucomoni contra, omnium haeredi bonorum, *cum*

*divitiae* jam *animos facerent,* auxit ducta in matrimonium Tanaquil, summo loco nata, et quae haud facile iis, in quibus nata erat, humiliora sineret ea, quae innupsisset.

When riches were *now* inspiring Lucomo, the heir of all the property, with lofty notions, Tanaquil, a lady of the highest extraction, increased those notions, and being one, moreover, who could not readily suffer the family into which she had married to remain inferior to that in which she had been born.— Lib. i. 34.

The two following sentences from Nepos resemble each other as closely as the pair just quoted, and are equally damaging to the doctrine or rather delusion of dependence.

In quo cum divitiis ornavit, tum etiam peritissimos belli navalis fecit Athenienses. Id quantae saluti *fuerit* universae Graciae, bello *cognitum* est Persico. Them. ii.

In his autem *cognitum* est quanto *antestaret* eloquentia innocentiae.

It would be easy to multiply many more examples combining the same conditions and establishing the same conclusions. It would be difficult, however, to get to the end of these examples before getting to the end of the reader's patience. Indeed, the examples already enumerated would have been more numerous than need required, had it not been that it is much more difficult to unlearn error, than to learn the simple truth at first.

# CHAPTER IV.

### THE THEORY OF THE "PREDICATE."

These three theories, the "Essential-part" theory, Grotefend and Forbiger's theory of the Conditional, the theory of "Dependence," have been discussed in turn, and, it is hoped, finally disposed of. Since all these theories have been devised to explain the same phenomenon, it might have been expected that they would bear some common affinity to each other. They are only like to each other in this, however, that they are utterly unlike the true theory of the subjunctive. The theory that yet remains to be examined, the theory of the "Predicate," remarkable in many respects, is also remarkable in this, that it bears no resemblance to the rest, except in so far that it resembles them by bearing no resemblance also to the true theory of the subjunctive. Equalling them in this respect, it far exceeds them in the extent to which it has perverted the logic of the Latin language, and marred the matchless beauty of its mechanism. Most men would be inclined to think that rules were made for language, but the Latin language, it would appear, has been made for the theory of the "predicate." Most men would be inclined to think that syntax ought always to be subordinate to the sense, but the sense of sentence after sentence has been offered up, without scruple or compunction, to this idol, not of the intellect, but of the imagination. If, indeed, its value were proportionate to the price which has been paid for it, it would be invaluable. But, probably, never before was so much given on the one side, and so little gotten on the other.

The three following sentences selected by Dr Carson, the author of the well-known treatise, *Qui, Quæ, Quod*, as illustrations of the theory of the "predicate," may be taken as a test of its value and truth. They are all taken from the same page (41), and therefore may be fairly regarded as specimens favourable to the display of the theory, rather than selections adverse to it, purposely made by a hostile critic. The first sentence is,—

Nec multo post cerva adfuit, quae ubera parvulo offerret.—Just. Here is its interpretation by Dr Carson,—

"And not long after a doe came up, which presented its dugs to the infant." And this is the interpretation, because the relative clause—quæ offerret—is said and supposed to contain the "predicate."

The true interpretation of the passage is this,—

The clause containing *quae offerret* is a most conspicuous and clear instance of a *purpose*, which the Latins appropriately enough express by the subjunctive. The doe *came up to present* her teats to the babe. Such provision had the gods, according to the ancient belief, made for the preservation of him who was destined to become the founder and father of the Roman empire.

Justin, who wrote the sentence quoted above, and all other Roman writers as well, wrote in blissful ignorance of the "predicate," for assuredly in this case it would have been folly to be wise. They were accustomed to acknowledge and render allegiance to the great law of logical consistency, but they knew nothing of the lawless license of caprice. This is still more manifest from the second of these three sentences.

Aderat, *qui nosceret*, Bacbius Massa, e procuratoribus Africae, jam tunc optimo cuique exitiosus.

"There was one Bebius Massa present who knew him, (one) of the governors of Africa, (and) fatally pernicious to every worthy character."—Tac.

Here it said and supposed that the relative clause —*qui nosceret*—contains the predicate of the sentence. Whatever may be the intrinsic value of this piece of information, it becomes by many degrees less than nothing, when once it is found how very great the price is which has been paid for it. The sense has again been sacrificed for the sake of imaginary syntax. The translator, blinded by love for his favourite theory, has missed the meaning of the sentence, and marred its true Roman symmetry and beauty.

Even in its maimed and mutilated form, divorced as it is from its most material members, to suit the theory of the predicate, the interpretation given raises serious doubts. But when once the main member of the sentence has been restored to its rightful place, the true meaning is manifest in a moment.

Nec multo post Piso interficitur: namque aderat qui nosceret, Bebius Massa e procuratoribus Africae, jam tunc optimo cuique exitiosus, et in causas malorum quae mox tulimus saepius rediturus.

Not long afterwards Piso also is slain, for Bebius was at hand ready *to recognise* him.—Tac. *Hist.*, lib. iv. 50.

The murderers of Piso, who were strangers to him, by mistaking in the dim twilight his slave for himself, had at first missed their victim. To preclude the possibility of a similar mistake a second time, Bebius Massa was at hand to point out to the pursuers their prey,—

Namque aderat, qui nosceret.

From the days of Daniel down to this day, it has always been deemed the chief end of an interpreter to explain, not to pervert, languages. If John Milton, who was Latin secretary during the Commonwealth, had mistified or mistaken the meaning of a despatch to or from His Highness Oliver Cromwell, it would scarcely have been deemed a sufficient and satisfactory excuse for him to have said that the "predicate was in the relative clause."

The last of the three illustrative specimens of the "predicate" is as follows:—

Praesto est qui neget rem ullam perspici posse sensibus.—Cic. It is stated (p. 13), "Logically, the relative clause must contain the *predicate*, not the *subject* of the sentence." It might be expected, then, that in the sentence just quoted, selected by Dr Carson as one containing all the conditions of the rule, the relative clause—qui neget—would contain the "predicate, not the subject of the sentence." That the reverse, however, is the case, may be proved by means of the definitions adopted by Dr Carson himself—"the predicate is that which is affirmed of the subject; the subject of a proposition is that concerning which anything is affirmed or denied."—P. 13. The only "subject of which anything is affirmed" in— Praesto est, qui neget rem ullam percipi posse sensibus—is,—*qui neget*, *i.e.*, the denier; and what is affirmed of him is,—he is at hand. The relative being identical with the antecedent expressed or understood must contain the "subject." Never was there a more unfortunate device than to invoke the aid of logic to the defence of the "theory of the predicate." Logic declines to be sponsor to that spurious offspring of erratic fancy. Logic asks what meaning there can be in saying or supposing that the predicate is in *qui neget*, unless it be meant that there is no predicate in *praesto* est. But there is just as much predication in *praesto est* as in *qui neget*. Therefore, the deliverance of logic is, that while predication is common to both clauses, the indicative as well as the subjunctive, it is the *peculiarity* of the predication alone that accounts for the subjunctive. What this *peculiarity* is will be stated distinctly in due course. There is yet another condition of the "theory of the predicate," which, though not more certainly fatal to it than the condition just disposed of, is more clearly so. To this condition Dr Carson attaches so much importance as to deem it indispensable to the operation of the theory, and insists on its presence again and again. At p. 5 he says, "We hesitate not to affirm, that when the subjects concerning which an assertion is to be made in the relative clause are vaguely and generally announced in that which precedes, the rule may be followed with safety and confidence. This *vagueness* or *indetermination* of the subject is, in fact, essential to the right application of the rule. When this is meant to be intimated the writer specifies no individuals, but contents himself with giving the name of that order of beings to which the subjects of his affirmation are declared to belong."

Again, at p. 6, he says, "It has been already stated, that to fulfil the conditions of this rule, the precise subjects to which the author alludes must be unknown to him and undefined."

And still further, p. 8, "So necessary is it to the proper application of this rule, that the subject should involve the conception of indetermination, and not convey a special import, that even the pronoun *quidam*, when it forms the subject of the declaration which follows it in the relative clause, is too definite to admit a subjunctive in the predicate."

There is one advantage attending Dr Carson's definiteness as to this indefiniteness in his "theory of the predicate." There can be no mistake as to his meaning. He has fairly and fully committed himself to the consequences of the doctrine of indefiniteness in connexion with the "theory of the predicate." There remains now no room either for retraction or retreat. A certain reviewer, who needs not now to be more specifically designated, has caught the same confident tone in defending the theory as Dr Carson himself. But what Dr Carson did by the renewed reiteration of a succession of sentences, that his champion has continued to compress into a single sentence, crowning and completing the work of self-destruction by the issue of a singularly foolish challenge. Speaking of the author, he says, "If he had wished to refute Dr Carson, the right method would have been to adduce *one* instance in a good classical author in which such expressions as *sunt qui* are joined with the indicative when the predicate is in the relative clause." Of course, in making this challenge, the reviewer was measuring the knowledge of others by his own. He asks one. He shall get more than he either asks or expects. The author will follow the liberal precedent of the Common Council of London, who, when asked by good Queen Bess to furnish fifteen ships and five thousand men against the Armada, furnished thirty ships and ten thousand men. The double of what has been asked will be given, and one more into the bargain. As three sentences of Dr

Carson's own selection, supposed to combine all the conditions of the theory, have been already given (with what result will be well remembered), so now three sentences will be given, which, though really combining all the conditions of the theory, yet, so far from containing a confirmation of it, contain the most certain and conspicuous violation of it which it is possible to contain. As Dr Carson requires and desires "the subjects concerning which an assertion is to be made in the relative clause are vaguely and generally announced in that which precedes," moreover, "the predicate is in the relative clause," further, as his champion, the reviewer requires and desires "the authors are good classical authors," and yet, after all, *sunt qui* is joined with the indicative.

The first passage is taken from Cæsar—

Rhenus autem oritur ex Lepontiis, qui Alpes incolunt, et longo spatio per fines Nantuatium, Helvetiorum, Sequanorum, Mediomatricorum, Tribocorum, Trevirorum citatus fertur, et ubi Oceano appropinquat, in plures defluit partis multis ingentibusque insulis effectis, quarum pars magna a feris barbarisque nationibus incolitur, ex quibus *sunt, qui* piscibus atque ovis avium vivere *existimantur*, multisque capitibus in Oceanum influit.—*De Bel. Gal.*, lib. iv. 10.

The second passage is taken from Sallust :—

*Sunt qui* ita *dicunt*, imperia ejus injusta, superba, crudelia, barbaros nequivisse pati.—*Cat.* xix.

The third passage is taken from Cicero,—

*Sunt qui*, quod sentiunt, non *audent* dicere.—*De Of.* i. 24.

Thus wrote Cæsar, Sallust, and Cicero, who, it may be presumed, knew how to use their own tongue. And yet Dr Carson wrote " We hesitate not to affirm, that when the subjects concerning which an assertion is to be made in the relative clause are *vaguely* and *generally* announced in that which precedes, the *rule may be followed with safety and confidence.*" Here is the rule, "The relative *qui, quae, quod,* after *sum, reperio, inveni, habeo, adsum, desum,* and some other verbs, is followed by the subjunctive mood."—Page 2. Farther on, Dr Carson says, speaking of a passage which was not in his opinion a fair illustration of his rule, " Now it is manifest that in this passage that condition of the rule is not complied with which requires the subject to be indeterminate, or, in other words, to consist of some members or other of *a class which are unknown to and cannot be specified by the speaker or writer.*"—P. 6, 7.

Of the three passages quoted above from Cæsar, Sallust, and Cicero, it cannot be said "that condition of the rule has not been complied with which requires the subject to be indeterminate," for what could be more indeterminate than—Sunt qui existimantur—*Sunt qui ita dicunt*—Sunt qui *audent;* yet these Latin writers did not come to the same conclusion as Dr Carson, for they used the indicative when he says the subjunctive ought to be used. But this is not all. It will be remembered that Dr Carson has said, as already quoted, "So necessary is it to the proper application of this rule, that the subject should involve the conception of indetermination, and not convey a special import, that even the pronoun *quidam*, when it forms the subject of the declaration which follows it in the relative clause, *is too definite to admit a subjunctive in the predicate.*"—P. 8. Now that Carson has been heard, it will be interesting as well as instructive to hear Cicero on this point. In his oration Pro L. Mur., the following passage is found,—

*Inventus est* scriba *quidam* Cn. Flavius qui cornicum oculos *confixerit*, et singulis diebus ediscendis fastos populo *proposuerit*, et ab ipsis cautis jurisconsultis eorum sapientiam *compilarit*. There was found one Flavius, a clerk, who transfixed the eyes of the crows, *i.e.*, cheated the cunning, or bit the biters; and published daily a list of court-days for the people to get by heart, and stole their knowledge from the crafty lawyers themselves.—Cap. xi.

This personage, Flavius, was quite well known to Cicero. He alludes to him again and again in his writings, *e.g.*, Ad. Att. vi. 1, 8, and De Or. i. 41. He, however, does not deem the epithet *quidam* by which he designates him "*too definite to admit a subjunctive in the predicate*," as Dr Carson did.

Thus the fact, that subjects consisting of a "class which are unknown to and cannot be specified by the writers," are found in the best Latin writers, contrary to the reiterated declaration of Dr Carson, finds its fitting counterpart in the fact that *quidam* is *not* too definite, contrary also to the declaration of Dr Carson, to admit of a predicate in the subjunctive. The rule, therefore, is just the reverse of what is right in all its requirements. The doctrine, that the numbers of a "class," whether known or unknown, have anything to do with the subjunctive, is a delusion. Just as it is not predication itself that has anything to do with the subjunctive, but only the *character* of predication, so it is not the numbers of a class whether known or unknown to the writer, but its *nature*, which has to do with the subjunctive. That this is true, will appear from the following series of sentences. In each of them the subject, though known and named by the writer, is followed by a relative with the subjunctive; hence the fact, that a "class which are unknown and cannot be specified by the writers," are also followed by a relative with the subjunctive, is a mere accident, so far as the point at issue is concerned, and can neither constitute the condition nor the cause of the subjunctive. The first sentence is taken from Cicero,—

Sapientia *est* enim *una, quae* moestitiam ex animis *pellat, quae* nos exhorrescere metu non *sinat.—De Fin.*, lib. i. 13.

The next, combining the same conditions and pointing to the same conclusion, is taken from Horace,—

Nil admirari prope res *est una*, Numici,
Solaque, quae *possit* facere et servare beatum.
—Lib. i., Ep. vi.

The next, taken from Ovid, remarkable in many

respects, will be referred to again at a more advanced stage of this argument,—

> *Una est*, quae *reparet*, seque ipsa reseminet ales,
> Assyrii Phoenica vocant: non fruge nec herbis
> Sed terris lacrymis et succo vivit amomi.
> —*Met.* xv. 319.

The two next, one from Nepos, the other from Cæsar, not to be the same, are as similar as is possible to those just given,—

Haec *altera* victoria *est*, quae cum Marathonio *possit* comparari tropaeo. Nam pari modo apud Salamina parvo numero navium *maxima post hominum memoriam* classis est divicta.—*Them.* c. 5.

*Erant* omnino itinera *duo*, quibus itineribus domo exire *possent*.—*De Bel. Gal.*, lib. i. 6.

The last sentence, like the first, is taken from Cicero,—

*Reperti sunt duo equites* Romani, *qui* te ista cura *liberarent*, et sese illa ipsa nocte paullo ante lucem me meo in lectulo interfecturos *pollicerentur*.—*Orat. in L. Cat.*, I. 4.

It will be remembered that *reperio* is one of those verbs, according to Dr Carson's rule as quoted above, which require the subjunctive, "when followed by no other predicate than the relative clause." It is quite true that the two knights are not "specified" by Cicero in this passage, but it was not because they "could not be specified as a class unknown." In another oration he distinctly designates one of them by name,—

Quibus ego rebus, judices, ita flectebar animo atque frangebar ut jam ex memoria quas mihi ipse fecerat insidias deponerem: ut jam immissum esse ab eo *C. Cornelium*, qui me in aedibus meis, in conspectu uxoris meae ac liberorum meorum *trucidaret*, obliviscerer.—*Orat. pro P. Sulla*, cap. vi.

That class of sentences, which this chapter takes cognisance of, and which the "theory of the predicate" has hitherto been supposed by many to comprehend, has puzzled and perplexed scholars ever since the study of the Latin language has become the subject of critical investigation and any attempt been made to present its syntax in a systematic and scientific form. One writer who has devoted himself to the subject, and who deserves to be accounted both able and accomplished, hath expressed himself thus,—" The author has devised no theory of his own to account for these facts; nor has he adopted that of any other writer." Another Scottish scholar, equally remarkable for his classical attainments and great general ability, has expressed himself to the following effect,—" There is a very subtle principle involved here; one which has never, so far as I am aware, been properly expounded in words, though it has been felt and acted up to by Latinists, both ancient and modern, in practice."

The most matured view of modern German scholars on the subject, coupled with the deliberate deliverance of one who may justly be regarded as a good representative of English philologists, is to be learned by a reference to the *Bibliotheca Classica*. Mr Long, of Trinity College, Cambridge, the editor, in a note on Cicero, *Orat. I. in L. Cat.*, cap. xii., thus writes,— "*Quanquam non nulli.* In this sentence there are 'qui —non videant, aut dissimulent,' and 'qui spem aluerunt — corroboraverunt.' Halm observes, that 'qui aluerunt' does not stand on the same line (staht nicht coordinirt) with 'qui videant,' which occupies the place of a predicate." He means that there are some persons of the class or kind of persons who do not see what is before them. Mr Long, after justly asserting that this explanation is neither sufficient nor satisfactory, proceeds to offer his own solution of the difficulty. He says, "It is only a Roman form of expression which requires the subjunctive in such cases. The indicative is used in the other part of the sentence, 'qui —aluerant,' simply, I think, because it is further removed from 'quanquam non nulli sunt,' and the speaker returns to the direct and usual form."

The author entertains the most sincere respect for the scholarly accomplishments of Mr Long, and he gladly embraces this opportunity of expressing his warm admiration for the true intellectual independence and fine speculative faculty of which this edition of Cicero bears the clearest and most conspicuous impress throughout; but he must be permitted to decline giving his assent to this solution of the difficulty. He, however, would not have ventured to characterize the solution as erroneous or defective, had he not been prepared with his proof.

Mr Long seems to think that it is only a peculiar Roman form of expression that requires the subjunctive in such cases. It will be found on further examination that there is nothing peculiar at all about the form of expression in question; that it is in perfect unison with the other usages of the subjunctive; that it is only a striking illustration of the essential unity of the subjunctive, and the exquisitely logical character of the Latin language.

It will be readily admitted that there is an essential unity between all the different usages of the three other moods in the Latin language,—the indicative, imperative, and infinitive. If any argument might be founded on analogy, the same essential unity that is characteristic of the other moods, might be expected à *priori* to be found in the subjunctive also. All the usages of three moods in the same language having been found to be consistent with each other, on a calculation of chances according to the doctrine of probabilities, it might fairly be presumed that the usages of the fourth would agree likewise. The actual result of an investigation will be found to justify the à *priori* calculation. The affinities between the various usages of the subjunctive, though at first sight somewhat *remote*, are not on that account the less *real*. The difference that divides them will diminish by degrees. Although different in form they are not discordant in their nature.

Probably, what makes the first and most forcible impression on the mind of a thoughtful student of the Latin language, is the practice of the Roman writers to report the sentiments or speech of another by means of the subjunctive. Nowhere else is the subjunctive so frequently found as in reported speech. This is the first and fundamental usage of the subjunctive, and its study will furnish the key to unlock the other mysteries connected with it. This peculiar function of the subjunctive imparts both flexibility and compass to the language, as a powerful and delicate instrument for the expression of human thought. An Englishman knows as well, as a Roman knew, the difference between rumour and authentic information; the difference between the evidence of hearsay and the evidence of personal observation in a court of justice; but the employment of the artificial sign of inverted commas is but a poor substitute for the regular Roman mode of reporting speech. That peculiar form of narration enabled a Roman to recount acts, for which he declined to be responsible, which he repudiated, and branded with his moral reprobation. Two illustrative specimens of this usage of the subjunctive, forming a connecting link between the other usages of this mood, are here selected, one from Cicero, the other from Quintilian.

The first is from Cicero,—

Aristides nonne ob eam causam expulsus est a patria, quod praeter modum justus *esset.*—*Tusc.* v. 36.

A passage from Nepos, bearing a close affinity to

this one from Cicero, ought to be extracted in connexion with it,—

Cui ille respondit se *ignorare* Aristidem, sed sibi non placere, quod ita cupide *elaborasset*, ut *praeter caeteros Justus appellaretur.—Arist.* i.

These passages prove that the Romans employed the subjunctive in reporting the speeches and sentiments of others, not only because they were not bound to believe them to be true, but believing them to be true they might *repudiate them as wrong.* Cicero, who had been consul during the Catilinarian conspiracy, and who would have been very glad to have got banished a certain citizen, that was too bad, had no sympathy with the Athenians, who banished a certain citizen because he was *too good—quod praeter modum justus esset.*

The cognate passage from Quintilian is,—

Socrates accusatus est, quod *corrumperet* juventutem et novas superstitiones *induceret.*—iv. 4.

Quintilian, by employing the subjunctives,—*corrumperet, induceret,*—in reporting the sentiments of the Athenians, intimates not only that he considered the charges to be false, but that he condemned the whole course of conduct pursued by the Athenians towards Socrates, remembering, no doubt, "that immortal page which tells how meekly and bravely the first great martyr to intellectual liberty took the cup from his weeping gaoler."

Probably few will be found who will not admit and admire the peculiar power of expression possessed by the Latin language in this usage of its subjunctive. With as much propriety and truth, however, and as little benefit to the understanding of the student, might it have been said in this case also, as in the case of *sunt qui dicant*, "the subjunctive contained the predicate." The two cases are virtually the same, as will now be proved for the first time.

In Livy, the following passage is found,—

Artena inde *Volscorum* oppidum, ab tribunis obsideri coepta. .... Diruta et arce et urbe Artena, reductae legiones ex Volscis, omnesque vis Romana Veios conversa est. .... *Sunt, qui* Artenam Veientium, non Volscorum, fuisse *credant*. *Praebet errorem*, quod ejusdem nominis urbs inter Caere atque Veios fuit: sed eam reges Romani delevere, *Caeretumque* non Veientium fuerat. Altera haec nomine eodem in *Volsco* agro fuit, cujus excidium dictum est.—Lib. iv. 61.

Here Livy employs the expression, *Sunt qui credant* = dicant. There is no peculiar virtue in *Sunt qui*— which of itself requires the subjunctive. It would be as good Latin to say *Sunt qui credunt*, as *Sunt qui credant*. But Livy employs the latter form of expression, rather than the first, because he believes that the historians who believe so—*credant*—are *wrong*. He says this in the very next sentence, *Praebet errorem*—in express terms, and then shows the reason why. Nor is this a single and solitary passage in Livy; similar ones are almost found in shoals. The only difficulty found is not in their scarcity, but in their selection. The next is taken from the tenth Book, — Ceterum antequam consules in Etruriam pervenirent, Senones *Galli* multitudine ingenti ad Clusium venerunt, legionem Romanam castraque oppugnaturi. Here Livy states what he believes to be *true*, and employs the indicative accordingly, —*Galli ad Clusium venerunt.* Farther on in his narrative he states,—*Sunt qui Umbros* fuisse, *non Gallos, tradant;* nec tantum cladis acceptum : et circumventis pabulatoribus cum L. Manlio Torquato legato Scipionem propraetorem subsidium e castris tulisse, victoresque *Umbros* redintegrato proelio victos, captivosque iis ac praedam ademptam. Here Livy, by employing the subjunctive—*tradant*—states a fact, for by the subjunctive the Latins stated a fact as frequently and as forcibly as they did by the indicative, whatever grammarians may have hitherto said to the contrary. It was an undoubted fact, that certain historians left a record; but Livy, by employing the subjunctive in *Sunt qui tradant,* implies that they left a record of what he believed to be *not true.* That this is the true, as well as the new, explanation of what has hitherto been regarded as mysterious, is proved by the very next sentence in the context of Livy. That historian thus proceeds,—

*Similius vero est,* a *Gallo* hoste, quam *Umbro,* eam cladem acceptam; quod, quum saepe alias, tum eo anno, *Gallici* tumultus, praecipuus terror civitatem tenuit. Itaque praeter quam quod ambo consules profecti ad bellum erant cum quattuor legionibus et magno equitatu Romano, Campanisque mille equitibus delectis, ad id bellum missis, et sociorum nominisque Latini majore exercitu, quam Romani ; *alii duo exercitus* haud procul urbe Etruriae oppositi, unus in Falisco, alter in Vaticano agro.—Cap. xxvi.

By the words *Similius vero est*, Livy expressly intimates, what was already as certainly, though not so clearly implied—in *sunt qui tradant*—that certain historians were *wrong* in stating it was the Umbrians, and not the Gauls, at whose hands the Romans had sustained a signal reverse in arms.

· But it is not after long intervals only in the historical work of Livy that this form of expression— *Sunt qui dicant*, tradant, scribant—occurs. It occurs again in this very chapter, and in such a way as to show that the idea associated with it was constantly before the mind of Livy, and that it possessed a common affinity with the other usages of the subjunctive. Nearer the commencement of the chapter he says—

Invenio apud quosdam, extemplo, consulatu inito, profectos in Etruriam Fabium Deciumque, sine ulla mentione sortis provinciarum certaminumque inter collegas, *quae exposui*. *Sunt, quibus* nec haec quidem certamina exponere satis *fuerit;* adjecerint et Appii criminationes de Fabio absente ad populum, etc.

This passage is remarkable in more respects than one. In the first place, it is fatal to Dr Carson's doctrine of indefiniteness, if indeed any further proof on that point were either necessary or desirable. The designation *apud quosdam* is definite, as the class indicated by *sunt quibus fuerit* is indefinite. Such a distinction never occurred to the mind of Livy. The historical method of each party in his estimation was wrong. The one—apud quosdam . . . sine ulla mentione—erred by defect; the other—*sunt quibus nec haec quidem certamina exponere satis fuerit: adjecerint* et Appii criminationes, etc., errs no less by excess.

In the second place, the passage proves that Livy has examined the writings of the historians to whom he refers so minutely, as to specify distinctly the particular points wherein he differs from them, where they say more than himself, and where they say less. How, then, consistently with probability or even with possibility can it be said, as Dr Carson has said, "This *vagueness* or *indetermination* of the subject is in fact essential to the right application of the rule. When this is meant to be intimated, the writer specifies no individuals, but contents himself with giving the name of that *order* of beings to which the subjects of his affirmation are declared to belong. Of some of the individuals of which it is composed, the assertion made in the relative clause will, he is confident, hold true, though what *those precise subjects are he neither knows nor professes to know*." Is it consistent with reason, that a historian, after having proved that other historians had recorded what was *not true*, and criticised them for having adopted a mode of narrative which was *not right*, should be represented as "neither knowing nor professing to know what these precise subjects were?" This conclusion, with all its consequences, must have been accepted by those who have hitherto accepted "the theory of the predicate."

There is another passage still stronger than any of these in Livy. The historian closes an elaborate description of a base and bloody deed, which stains the annals of the second Punic war, with this remark,—Haec *vera* fama est. Then two sentences follow, the first words of each of which are *Sunt qui*, followed by a subjunctive.

The reader of Livy will readily remember, when reminded, that one Flavius, a Lucanian, the head of those tribes that had continued faithful to Rome, himself now meditating a revolt to Hannibal, repaired to the Roman commander, T. S. Gracchus, representing that he had persuaded the heads of all the tribes that had revolted to Hannibal to return to their former allegiance to Rome, and that they at an appointed place, close at hand, only waited his presence to ratify the compact. Livy proceeds:—

Gracchus, fraudem et sermoni et rei abesse ratus, ac similitudine veri captus, cum lictoribus ac turma equitum e castris profectus, duce hospite in insidias praecipitatur. Hostes subito exorti: et, ne dubia proditio esset, Flavius his se adjungit. tela undique in Gracchum atque equites conjiciuntur. Gracchus ex equo desilit. idem ceteros facere jubet, hortaturque, ut, quod unum reliquum fortuna fecerit, id coho-

nestent virtute. Reliquum autem quid esse paucis,
a multitudine in valle silva ac montibus septa circumventis, practer mortem? id referre, utrum, prae-
bentes corpora, pecorum modo inulti trucidentur, an,
toto animo a patiendo exspectandoque eventu in impetum atque iram verso, agentes audentesque, per-
fusi hostium cruore, inter exspirantium inimicorum
cumulata armaque et corpora cadant. Lucanum
proditorem ac transfugam omnes peterent. qui eam
victimam prae se ad inferos misisset, eum decus exi-
mium egregiumque solatium suae morti inventurum.
Inter haec dicta paludamento circum laevum brachium
intorto (nam ne scuta quidem secum extulerant), in
hostes impetum fecit. Major, quam pro numero
hominum, editur pugna. jaculis maxime aperta corpora Romanorum, et, quum undique ex altioribus
locis in cavam vallem conjectus esset, transfiguntur.
Gracchum, jam nudatum praesidio, vivum capere
Poeni nituntur. ceterum ille, conspicatus Lucanum
hospitem inter hostes, adeo infestus confertos invasit,
ut parci ei sine multorum pernicie non posset. Exa-
nimem eum Mago extemplo ad Hannibalem misit,
ponique cum captis simul fascibus ante tribunal im-
peratoris jussit. *Haec vera fama est.* Gracchus in
Lucanis ad campos, qui Veteris vocantur, periit.

Gracchus imagining that the speech and act were
alike free from guile, and deceived by the appearance
of truth, accompanied by his lictors and a squadron
of cavalry, started from the camp. Under the conduct
of his professing friend, he is drawn into an ambus-

cade with headlong haste. The enemy suddenly spring to their feet, and lest the betrayal should seem to admit of doubt, Flavius attaches himself to them. Darts descend in showers on Gracchus and his men. Gracchus dismounting from his horse, and commanding his comrades to do the same, desires them to signalize by their bravery the last chance which fate had left them. And what but death, he said, was left to a few when encompassed by a host in a valley girt by hills and woods. But it made a great difference, whether like sheep yielding their bodies to the slayer, they died unavenged, or, turning their minds wholly away from passive endurance and the apprehension of their doom, to resistance and aggression, by doing deeds of daring, at last covered with their blood, they fell amid the accumulated armour and bodies of their dying foes. They ought, he said, to aim at the Lucanian traitor and apostate, for whosoever sent him as a victim before himself to the shades below, would thereby win a rare distinction and a glorious satisfaction for his own death. Having already, in the course of this speech, wrapped his military cloak round his left arm (for they had not so much as brought out their shields), he now rushes against the foe. A more severe encounter ensues than might have been expected from the number of the combatants. The bodies of the Romans were peculiarly exposed to the darts, and, as these were hurled from the higher grounds on all sides into the hollow valley below, were pierced through and through. The Carthaginians attempted to take Gracchus alive, who was by this time deprived of his body guard. But he, having discovered his Lucanian guest-friend among the foe, charged the crowded ranks with such fury, that he could not be spared without the sacrifice of many. Mago despatched his lifeless body at once to Hannibal, and ordered it, with the insignia of office taken at the same time, to be placed before the judgment-seat of that commander. This is the *true* tradition. Gracchus fell in Lucania near the "ancient" fields, as they are called.—Lib. xxv. 16.

Livy having thus recounted the circumstances connected with the death of Gracchus with extraordinary minuteness, sums up by saying, Haec *vera fama est.* He then proceeds to give the accounts of others by saying, Sunt *qui ostendant;* and by employing the subjunctive—*ostendant,* he leaves the inevitable and irresistible inference to be drawn, that he deemed these accounts altogether wrong.

*Sunt, qui* in agro Beneventano, prope Calorem fluvium, *ostendant,* a castris cum lictoribus ac tribus servis lavandi causa progressum, quum forte inter salicta innata ripis laterent hostes, nudum atque inermem, saxisque, quae volvit amnis, propugnantem, interfectum.

There are *those who represent,* that he, accompanied by his lictors and three slaves, having advanced a short way from the camp for the purpose of bathing, in the territory of Beneventum, near the river Calor, while the enemy chanced to be concealed in the brushwood on its banks, fell defending himself bravely with the stones he found in the stream.—Cap. 17.

Moreover, in the very next sentence the very same form of expression is found, charged with the very same significant meaning,—*Sunt qui scribant*, *i.e.*, the narrative is different from that of Livy, and altogether wrong.

*Sunt, qui,* haruspicum monitu quingentos passus a castris progressum, uti loco puro ea, quae ante dicta prodigia sunt, procuraret, ab insidentibus forte locum duabus turmis Numidarum circumventum *scribant*. As a Roman writer by employing the subjunctive in such a combination as *sunt qui dicant, scribant,* etc., intends to imply his dissent and disapproval, so he, as might have been expected, when he intends to imply his assent and approval employs the indicative. Livy also supplies this compliment of the proof.

Eorum *magis sententiae sum, qui,* Corniculo capto, Servii Tullii, qui princeps in illa urbe fuerat, gravidam viro occiso uxorem, cum inter reliquas captivas cognita casct, ob unicam nobilitatem ab regina Romana prohibitam *ferunt* servitio partum Romae edidisse, Prisci Tarquinii domo.—Lib. i. 39.

Of course, there is just as much predication in— qui *ferunt*—as there would have been in—qui *ferant;* but Livy, wishing to intimate his assent and approval of the narrative of an "indefinite class," accordingly employs the indicative.

But it is not Livy only among Roman writers, whose writings throw light on the true theory of this combination, although perhaps they have contributed more than those of any other. Tacitus associated the same idea with the combination as Livy. The following passage from the former is as conclusive and decisive as any that has been adduced from the latter:—

Paulo Fabio, Lucio Vitellio, consulibus, post longum saeculorum ambitum avis phoenix in Ægyptum venit, praebuitque materiam doctissimis indigenarum et Graecorum multa super eo miraculo disserendi: de quibus congruunt, et plura ambigua sed cognitu non absurda, promere libet: sacrum soli id animal, et ore ac distinctu pinnarum a coeteris avibus diversum, consentiunt qui formam ejus definiere: *de numero annorum varia traduntur: maxime vulgatum quingentorum spatium: sunt qui asseverent, mille quadringentos sexaginta unum intergici*, prioresque alites Sesoside primum, post Amaside dominantibus, dein Ptolemaeo qui ex Macedonibus tertius regnant, in civitatem cui Heliopolis nomen advolavisse, multa ceterarum volucrum comitatu novam faciem mirantium: Sed antiquitas quidem obscura.—*Annal.*, vi. 18.

Tacitus here states that while naturalists and historians agree as to the appearance of the phœnix, they differ as to the length of its life—consentiunt qui formam ejus definiere—de numero annorum varia traduntur. He, however, says that the common, and therefore probably the correct tradition, relative to the length of its life, was that it extended over a period of five hundred years — maxime vulgatum quingentorum spatium. On the other hand, he, as Livy would have done, represents the believers in that tradition, in whose favour few were found, which makes the period of fourteen hundred and sixty-one years elapse between the visit of a phœnix to Heliopolis — mille quadringentos sexaginta unum interjici — as expressing their opinion by the subjunctive — *sunt qui asseverent*. Herodotus, whom Tacitus probably read before writing the passage quoted above, represents the Heliopolitans themselves as saying that the period in question was five hundred years.

Και γαρ δη και στανιος επιφοιτα σφισι, δια ετεων (ως 'Ηλιουπολιται λεγουσι) τυτακοσιων. Φοιται δε τοτε φασι, ετεαν οι αποθανη ο πατηρ. — *Eut.*, 73.

The practice of Sallust coincides with that of Livy and Tacitus. *Fuere ea tempestate qui dicerent*, Catilinam, oratione habita, cum ad jusjurandum populares sceleris sui adigeret, *humani corporis sanguinem*, vino permixtum, in pateris circumtulisse. . . . *Nonnulli ficta et haec*, et multa praeterea, *existimabant*, ab his, qui Ciceronis invidium, quae postea orta est, leniri credebant atrocitate sceleris eorum, qui poenas dederant. Nobis ea res pro magnitudine *parum comperta est.*—*Cat.* xxii.

A person who had never heard of the "theory of the predicate" would not think of the "vagueness or indetermination of the subjects" in the reference— *Fuere qui dicerent*, Catilinam, *humani corporis* sanguinem circumtulisse,—but of the small number who would say, or the still fewer number that would believe, that a boy had been slain for the performance of a barbarous and inhuman rite. And so the contemporaries of Cataline and Sallust thought. Nay, more, not a few thought the allegation was a pure fiction,—Nonnulli haec ficta existimabant. Sallust, himself, intimates that the existence of the feeling expressed by the indicative—existimabant—was very natural. On the other hand, by the employment of the subjunctive in—Fuere qui dicerent,—he intimates the improbability of the unnatural allegation introduced by it, or, at all events, that he is not responsible for it. There never was a clearer or more certain illustration of the principle peculiar to reported sentiment or speech. But who ever yet heard of the theory of the predicate in connexion with reported speech?

It will be remembered that at an earlier stage of this argument, in answer to the foolish challenge of the reviewer, an instance of *Sunt qui* with the indicative, with the predicate, moreover, on the relative clause, as the phrase is, was adduced from Sallust. And never in any case was wisdom more justified of her children. Never was the logic of the Latin language more clearly and more certainly displayed. The passage previously quoted is as follows:—

Sed is Piso, in provincia ab equitibus Hispanis, quos in exercitu ductabat, iter faciens occisus est. *Sunt qui* ita *dicunt*, imperia ejus injusta, superba, crudelia, barbaros nequivisse pati: alii autem, equites illos, Cn. Pompeii veteres fidosque clientes voluntate ejus Pisonem adgressos; nunquam Hispanos praeterea tale facinus fecisse, sed imperia saeva multa antea perpessos. Nos eam rem *in medio relinquemus.—Cat.*, xix.

As each of the two alternatives possesses a fair show of probability in its favour, and as Sallust's information was not so positive as to say which was right, which was wrong, he merely leaves the point undetermined—*in medio*.

On the other hand, if his opportunity, or his faculty of observation, or his faculty of inference had been equal to those of Livy, and enabled him to say, " praebet errorem," " similius vero est," " haec vera est fama," he would have written—Sunt qui dicant.

It will also be remembered that an example of *Sunt qui* with the indicative, combining also the condition of the predicate in the relative clause, as the phrase is, was cited from Cicero :—

*Sunt* enim *qui*, quod sentiunt, etsi optimum sit, tamen invidiae metu non *audent* dicere.—*De Of.*, i. 25.

There are many persons who, from want of firmness of character and moral courage, dare not give expression to their sentiments, however excellent. This habit is not by any means strange; and Cicero, by employing the indicative in describing the individuals to whom it is peculiar, does not thereby visit it with his censure. With what difference of design he employs the subjunctive in the same combination, may be seen from the following sentence :—

## THE THEORY OF THE "PREDICATE." 101

Hic, *hic sunt*, in nostro numero, patres conscripti, in hoc orbis terrae sanctissimo gravissimoque consilio, *qui* de nostro omnium interitu, *qui* de hujus urbis atque adeo de orbis terrarum exitio *cogitent.*—*Orat.* I. *in L. Cat.*, iv.

It is not a common and certainly not a constitutional custom for senators to plot the ruin of their country. There is a great difference between those—qui non, metu invidiae, quod sentiunt, dicere *audent*, —and those—qui de urbis atque de orbis exitio *cogitent.* Cicero expresses the difference by employing a different mood in their description, the indicative in describing a habit common and not culpable, the subjunctive in describing a habit culpable and not common.

Nor had Cæsar a less sufficient or satisfactory reason for employing the indicative with Sunt qui than Cicero and Sallust,—Ex quibus *sunt qui* piscibus atque ovis avium vivere *existimantur.*—*De Bel. Gal.*, iv. 10.

Although this passage is not more certainly fatal to the theory of the predicate than any of the others that have been quoted, yet probably no other passage could be cited more clearly fatal to that theory, so clearly does it show the common-sense considerations by which the Romans were influenced alone in their employment of the indicative and subjunctive moods. They were influenced by common-sense considerations, and not by the arbitrary connexion or combination of words. The passage just quoted combines all the conditions deemed indispensable by the believers of the theory for its adequate display, yet Caesar, who was a stranger to these conditions, but did homage to the ordinary and obvious considerations of common sense, directly violates it. The indispensable condition of "vagueness and indetermination" is complied with in feris barbaresque nationibus ex quibus *sunt qui;* and the equally indispensable condition of the predicate being found in the relative clause, is complied with in qui existimantur, as the believers of the theory understand that phrase; and yet after all Caesar employs the indicative, *existimantur.* Caesar, who knew nothing of the "theory of the predicate," but knowing that "eggs and fish" are very good fare everywhere, and that nothing was more natural than that islanders (insulis quarum pars a feris nationibus incolitur) especially should subsist on them, accordingly very appropriately in referring to this practice employs the indicative. On the other hand, if Caesar had referred to a practice which he either felt disposed to discredit as improbable, or to disapprove of as improper, he would accordingly, in consistency with the genius of the Latin language, have employed the subjunctive. So consistent is the logical character of the Latin language throughout, and so copious is its literature, that it is possible to furnish from Cicero the exact complement of the picture presented by Caesar. The latter, in describing the diet of an uncivilized race of islanders, which he sees no reason to *criticise* either as *strange,* or to *condemn as wrong,* appropriately employs the indicative. The former, in describing the habits of a class of sensualists at table, which he at once considers *very strange*, and condemns as very *wrong*, appropriately employs the subjunctive :—

Nolim enim mihi fingere asotos, ut soletis, *qui* in mensam *vomant*, et qui de conviviis *auferantur*, crudique postridie se rursus *ingurgitent*.—*De Fin.*, lib. ii. 8.

Horace is the last Latin writer in connexion with whose name it has been deemed desirable to discuss and dispose of "the theory of the predicate." The bard of Venusia has proved a sad puzzle to believers in "the theory of the predicate." Nowhere else, as they allege, are exceptions to the "rule" more numerous than in his works. Of him Dr Carson thus speaks in reference to the "rule,"—

" Of all the authors of the classic poets whose works have been transmitted to us, Horace is *most guilty of violating the obligations of the general rule.*"—*Qui, Quae, Quod,* p. 29.

The believers in the "theory" of course plead in its defence, that exceptions prove the rule. There is, however, a limit to this line of defence. Whenever the exceptions to a rule are as numerous as its exemplifications, there is good ground for believing that there is no "rule" at all. Among the Roman writers, at least, there was no "rule" which required the subjunctive after the combination *sunt qui* of itself, apart from the peculiar sense desired and designed to be conveyed by the writer. From a vast number of passages quoted above, taken from very various prose writers, it has been seen that sunt qui dicunt is in every way as good Latin as sunt qui dicant; and Horace no more violated any law of the Latin language, whatever he may have done in the imagination of modern theorists, when he wrote—sunt quos *juvat*—sunt quibus unum opus *est*—est qui *spernit*,— than when he wrote—sunt qui scripta foro *recitent* —sunt qui *nolint* tetigisse—sunt qui *venentur* avaras. Horace employed the indicative or subjunctive according to the sense desired and required.

The ideas which he associated respectively with the indicative and subjunctive, in strict consistency with the exquisitely logical character of the Latin language, are as distinctly expressed by him as by Livy himself. In the following passage he indicates his meaning by the subjunctive in a manner not to be mistaken:—

Nec recito cuiquam nisi amicis, idque coactus,
Non ubivis coramve quibus libet. In medio *qui*
Scripta foro *recitent sunt*, multi quique laevantes.—
Lib. i., Sat. iv. 73.

Horace here, with the modesty of true genius, and with the taste of a gentleman, states that it was his custom to read aloud the productions of his muse in private, not in public, to a favoured few, not to fortuitous comers, and that, too, only by constraint, and not by choice. Moreover, he compares, or rather contrasts, the contrary custom of other poets or poetasters, and contrasting, of course condemns, who recited their verses indiscriminately in the market-place and in the bath-room. Nothing was more natural for Horace, who like other Roman writers, employing the subjunctive in reporting a speech or sentiment, for which he was not responsible, and wished to repudiate, than to employ the subjunctive also in describing an *act* which he desired and designed thereby to repudiate,—*Sunt qui* scripta foro *recitent.* What the believers in the " theory of the predicate" would say here is, that "the predicate is in the relative clause,"—*qui recitent.* This assertion might possibly have some point or sort of meaning if there were no predicate in *sunt.* But in this and similar sentences there is as much predication in the indicative *sunt* as in the subjunctive *recitent. Predication is no more peculiar to the subjunctive than to the indicative. It is only the character of predication which at once constitutes the clear condition and certain cause of the subjunctive.*

The next passage presents the same characteristics, and points to the same conclusions as the preceding one,—

> Pars hominum gestit conducere publica : *sunt qui*
> Crustis et promis viduas *venentur* avaras,
> *Excipiantque* senes, quos in vivaria mittant.—
> 
> *Ep.*, lib. i. 77.

The ambition to farm the public revenues of Rome, by which Horace in the first line of this extract represents a certain class as actuated, was an honourable ambition. The "publicani" numbered among themselves far more equestrian than plebeian names. The term "publicanus" at Rome, whatever it may have been among the provinces in general, and in Palestine in particular, was regarded as a term of respect and not reproach. Reproach, but not respect, however, Horace reserves for the class referred to next. Equally opposed to the "publicani," and odious to Horace, was the class of fortune-hunters. *Sunt qui* viduas *veneniur* avaras—*excipiantque* senes. He rebukes their conduct by the employment of the subjunctive, in the same way that he would have repudiated their sentiments by the employment of that mood in reported speech.

The following extract also contains the combination of *sunt qui* followed by a subjunctive, by means of which Horace, no less certainly and conspicuously than in the preceding passage, condemns the conduct of a class:—

*Sunt qui nolint* tetigisse nisi illas
Quarum subsuta talos tegat instita veste.—

Lib. i., Sat. ii. 28.

Thus far the passages quoted from Horace have contained instances only of *sunt qui* followed by the subjunctive. The following extract, equally instructive and decisive of the point at issue, presents the striking peculiarity of containing one line which combines both constructions; in the first part of the line *sunt qui* with the subjunctive, in the latter part *est qui* with the indicative:—

Gemmas, marmor, ebur, Tyrrhena sigilla, tabellas,
Argentum, vestes Gaetulo murice tinctas,
*Sunt qui* non *habeant, est qui* non *curat* habere.—
Lib. ii., Ep. ii. 182.

Of the numerous passages which have been cited in contravention of the "theory of the predicate," perhaps none could be named more clearly and completely fatal to it than this. It cannot be said that *est qui* non *curat* is an inadvertency, for in the immediately preceding clause Horace wrote *sunt qui* non *habeant*. If there were any virtue in the syntax *sunt qui* apart from the sense, such as to require the subjunctive at the commencement of a line, surely the same syntax would require the same mood at the close of the line. But there is, of course, no virtue in the syntax *sunt qui*, apart from the sense, such as to require the subjunctive. Horace wrote *habeant* after *sunt qui*, because the sense required it, and with no less propriety he wrote *curat* after est qui, because the sense required it. The believers, however, in the "theory of the predicate," suppose that Horace, in writing *curat* instead of "*curet*," violated a fundamental "rule" of the Latin language. But so far is this from being the case, that if he had written "*curet*," he would have written contrary to the genius of the Latin language, contrary to the practice of the best Latin writers, and to his own practice elsewhere. The subjunctive in *sunt qui non habeant* is not more in accordance with the subjunctives in similar combinations which have been cited from Cicero and Caesar, Sallust and Livy, than the indicative in *est qui non curat* is in accordance with the indicatives which have been cited from these writers:—

*Sunt qui,* quod sentiunt, metu invidiae non *audent* dicere.
*Sunt qui* piscibus atque ovis avium vivere *existimantur.*
*Sunt qui* ita *dicunt* imperia ejus injusta nequivisse pati.

Horace, by employing the subjunctive in the clause, Sunt qui non *habeant,* implied that those who had not great wealth were *dissatisfied* with their condition, and thereby intimated his condemnation of their conduct. On the other hand, by employing the indicative in the clause, Est qui non *curat* habere, he implied that the *wise* man has not costly possessions, and does not wish to have,—thereby contrasting his conduct with the opposite class, and by contrasting it he commends it:—

Sunt qui non *habeant,* est qui non *curat* habere.

The following additional passages from Horace are cited in confirmation of this interpretation of *est qui* non *curat.* They are cited by Dr Carson for a very different purpose. He says, "The following are all, or nearly all, the passages in which Horace is chargeable with a deliberate infringement of the general rule," p. 30, *Qui, Quae, Quod.* They are supposed to violate the imaginary "theory of the predicate." It is quite possible they may violate the "general rule" as known to believers in "the theory of the predicate," since no such "rule" was known to the Latins, but they illustrate a general rule which the Latins delighted to recognise and respect. The first passage is:—

*Sunt* quorum ingenium nova tantum crustula *promit*,
Nequaquam satis in re una consumere curam.
*Ser.*, lib. ii. 4, 47.

The reader of Horace will readily remember that he puts the assertion thus quoted into the mouth of one Catius. This Catius, distinguished for devotion to his belly, in a treatise on his favourite passion, had thus spoken of himself, "Haec primus invenit et cognovit Catius Miltiades." Catius would appear to have been among the Romans, what the chef of Leo X. was among the French, who got the name of Jean de Careme, for a soup-maigre which he invented for the Pope, and what Florence was among the English, who, chef to successive Dukes of the House of Buccleuch, is immortalized by Scott as the inventor of the *potage à la Meg Merrilies*. Since Catius, then, plumed himself on his inventive ingenuity, nothing could be conceived as more natural than that he should say:—

*Sunt quorum* ingenium nova tantum crustula *promit*, i.e., There are those whose genius produces some new kind of pastry only.

Catius, of course, refers to himself, and, of course, with approbation. The indicative is, therefore, accurately and appropriately employed. Dr Carson thought that therein "Horace" was chargeable with a deliberate infringement of the general "rule." Had Horace, however, written as Dr Carson would have desired him, he would have written not according to, but against the general rule of the Latin language.

The next passage is the well-known

> *Sunt quos* curriculo pulverem Olympicum,
> Collegisse *juvat*.

*Sunt quos juvat* is another instance of what Dr Carson has called a deliberate infringement of the "general rule," and what Dr Parr and his faithful followers have hitherto considered to be correctly so-called. Since the character of an act is often best determined by its consequences, it will be instructive to see what would have been the consequence, if Horace, in this instance, had complied with the "general rule" as it is called. If Horace had written sunt quos *juvet* instead of sunt quos juvat, he would thereby have placed those who are referred to in that combination on an equality with those who are referred to in the following combinations:—

> In medio *qui*
> Scripta foro recitent *sunt*, multi quique lavantes.
> *Sunt qui*
> Crustis et pomis viduas *venentur* avaras,
> *Excipiantque* senes, quos in vivaria *mittant*.

That is to say, the practical application of "the theory of the predicate" makes Horace place "fortune-hunters, and poetasters, who recite their verses in the market-place and the bath-room," in the same category as "charioteers in the Olympic race-course," whom Pindar, a brother bard, has praised in poetry which will perish only when the music of eloquence and of song shall have ceased to charm the minds of men. Such is the theory of the predicate. As a tree is tested by its fruit, so a theory ought to be tested by its fruit also.

The remaining passage from Horace containing, as it is supposed, a deliberate infringement of the general rule, is as follows:—

*Sunt quibus* unum opus *est* intactae Palladis urbem,
Carmine perpetuo celebrare et
Undique dicerptam fronte praeponere olivam.
—*Car.*, lib. i. 7, 7.

After what has been said on the preceding passages, there will be no need of any elaborate statement or argument to prove that Horace here was wiser than his critics. Nothing is more notorious or natural than the universal feeling which nativity excites. There is no place, the plainest as well as the most picturesque, which does not possess peculiar charms in the eyes of its natives. Athens, "the eye of Greece," conspicuous among cities for the beauties of nature and art, was more remarkable for nothing than the production of patriotic poets, who loved to sing her praise. No practice could possibly have been more remote from what was strange or wrong. It would have been both strange and wrong, however, if Horace had entertained an opposite opinion, and he would have entertained an opposite opinion, had he expressed himself by employing the subjunctive:—

*Sunt quibus* unum opus *sit.*

But Horace, conceding to his brother bards of Greece the right to praise the land of their birth in preference to every other, while claiming for himself a similar right respecting Italy:—

Hanc veniam petimusque damusque vicissim,

with a perfect knowledge at once of the great law of toleration, and of the general laws of the Latin language, wrote:—

*Sunt quibus* unum opus *est* intactae Palladis urbem.
Carmine perpetuo celebrare.

Horace, partly because of the license by which poets are said to dispense with laws, partly because of his alleged partiality for Greek constructions, has been singled out for special condemnation in connexion with the "predicate." With as much propriety and truth might Cicero have been selected for a similar purpose. Horace did nothing in connexion with the syntactical combination in question, which Cicero did not do. Cicero, who is not likely to be charged with a propensity to indulge in poetical license, or a partiality for Greek constructions, like Horace, only wrote in accordance with the principle, that the syntax must be subordinate to the sense. Cicero, like Horace, wrote *sunt qui dicunt*—as readily as *sunt qui dicant*—when the sense so required, that is, whenever he desired to express an *ordinary fact, what the understanding could not regard as strange, nor conscience condemn as wrong*,—*e.g.*,

*Sunt qui*, quod sentiunt, etsi optimum sit, tamen invidiae metu non *audent* dicere.—*De Of.*, lib. i. 25.

On the other hand, whenever Cicero desired and designed to describe an *extraordinary fact, what either the understanding regarded as strange, or the conscience condemned as wrong*, then, like Horace, he employed *Sunt qui* with the subjunctive,—*e.g.*,

*Sunt qui* suum se negotium agere *dicant*, ne facere cuiquam videantur injuriam.—*De Of.*, lib. i. 29.

That this is the true as well as new explanation of the syntactical combination *Sunt qui*, that which constitutes the clear condition and certain cause of the subjunctive following it, is proved by the fact, that this usage of the subjunctive is clearly and closely allied to the subjunctive of reported speech, which was primarily and properly employed, when a writer declining to be responsible for what he considered strange, or believed to be wrong in the speech or sentiments of another, thereby repudiated them,—*e.g.*,

Nonne Aristides ob eam causam expulsus est a patria, quod *praeter modum* justus *esset*.—Cic. *Tusc.*, v. 36.

Socrates accusatus est, quod *corrumperet* juventutem, et novus superstitiones *induceret.*—Quintil., iv. 4.

Never, probably, was there a theory more devoid of a principle on which to rest, more opposed to all analogy, than the theory of the "predicate." The paramount principle by which the Romans were regulated in their written compositions was, that the syntax should be subordinate to the sense. With them the sense always determined the shape of the sentence. The Romans never sacrificed the end to the means. The reverse, however, is the case with the theory of the "predicate." According to that theory, in the sentence,—he slew the first man he met—the "predicate is in the relative clause." For the meaning is not he slew the first man, *i.e.*, Adam, but the first man that he met. Yet a Roman would never have written,—

Occidit primum hominem, quem *videret;*

He would have written,—

Occidit hominem, quem primum *vidit.*

The conditions chosen by its own supporters prove that the theory is altogether false, and foreign to the language of the Romans. So far from fulfilling the first function of a theory, throwing light on language, it has been seen that it mars its form, and mystifies its meaning. It is thus worse than useless. One class of sentences it misinterprets, another it represents as written in bad Latin. With as much propriety and truth might it have represented *ut* or *quin* with the indicative as bad Latin, since they are most commonly found with the subjunctive, as it has represented *sunt qui* with the indicative to be bad Latin, since *sunt qui* is more commonly found with the subjunctive. As if there were no difference of sense to explain the difference of syntax! As if the indicative had not usages as peculiar and proper to it as the subjunctive has! It is stated, p. 2, *Qui, Quae, Quod,* "instead of *sunt qui* dicant, we may say *dicunt* merely; *i.e., homines nonnulli dicunt.*" This is a great delusion. To say that the one expression is equal to the other, is to say that the subjunctive is equal to the indicative. The meaning of *nonnulli dicunt* is, some, *i.e., not many,* say. The meaning of *sunt qui dicant* is, *there are those who say, either what is strange, or what is wrong, what the writer is not responsible for, and repudiates accordingly.*

It is obvious that the same fallacy, which has been exposed in the case of the "essential part theory," Grotefend and Forbiger's "theory of the conditional," the theory of "dependence," is common to the theory of the "predicate." *Est qui* or *sunt qui* has been supposed to be an essential of the subjunctive. It is, however, a mere accident, bearing no affinity whatever to what constitutes the clear condition and certain cause of the subjunctive. This confusion between an accident and an essential, has been the cause of all the inconsistencies and absurdities which have sprung from the adoption of the theory of the "predicate." These, it has been seen, have been neither few in number, nor light in their nature. And such a result might have been anticipated, where a principle, on which to found the theory, and analogy to support it, were only conspicuous by their absence, and their absence seemed only to be compensated by the presence of a pertinacious purpose to maintain the theory at any expense whatever. The price paid on the one hand is the stultification of the Roman writers, and the mystification of their readers, the gain on the other hand to the academic world is, the information that "the predicate is in the relative clause." The meaning of Cicero and Tacitus is destroyed, Horace is charged with the perpetration of bad Latin, and the consolatory compensation is "obedience has been paid to the 'law,' to the 'general rule.'" Extraordinary as the process of balancing may seem, it is not entirely without a precedent or a parallel. Scientific and historical readers will remember, when reminded, that, on a certain occasion, a pertinacious theorist said:—

"I stand up for Artemius. That he killed his patient is plain enough. But still he acted quite according to rule. A man dead is a man dead, and there is an end of the matter. But if rules are to be broken, there is no saying what consequences may follow."

The historical reader will remember the old German officer, who, reviling Napoleon for spoiling the art of war, just as the propounders of the theory of the "predicate" have reviled Horace for marring the beauty of the Latin language, said,—"In my youth we used to march and countermarch all the summer without gaining or losing a square league, and then we went into winter quarters. And now comes an ignorant, hot-headed young man, who flies about from Boulogne to Ulm, and from Ulm to the middle of Moravia, and fights battles in December. The whole system of his tactics is monstrously incorrect!"

Whatever satisfaction the propounders of the theory of the "predicate" may have derived from the belief "that the law is uniformly respected by prose writers," though at the expense of mystifying their meaning, and marring the beauty of their periods, the dictate of common sense is that the end of theories is to explain language, that those which fail to fulfil this their first condition, fail altogether, and become positively pernicious.

There can be little doubt that the "patronage" vouchsafed by Dr Parr, to the theory of the "predicate," has contributed largely to its general adoption. Whatever may be the correct explanation of his sanction of it, the most charitable one is, that he had not given that consideration to the subject which its difficulty demanded, and its importance deserved. No amount of human skill, though exercised to the utmost extent by the most accomplished advocate, could save it from the doom it deserves. Its most adequate and appropriate description is to be found in the well-known words of the late Lord Denman—

"It is a delusion, a mockery, and a snare." Extending over a period of fifty years, it has done more than any other theory to conceal the logic of the Latin language and the true theory of the subjunctive. Flowing from the fancy, and not from the understanding, it has flashed fitfully before the eyes of the student, but furnished no steady light to guide him in his darkness and difficulty. It will find no fixed place in the firmament of human discovery. As the noble fabric of the Latin language was framed by master hands, long ere the theory of the "predicate" floated in the fancy of its prime projector, so it will continue to form by simple laws the taste of youth, long after that theory shall have faded from the minds of men.

# CHAPTER V.

### THE FUNCTION OF *UT*.

It is very easy to see why *ut*, introducing a purpose, which it so often does in Latin, should be followed by the subjunctive. Inasmuch as the purpose or project may be a wild or wicked one, and therefore not deserving of accomplishment, or inasmuch as the purpose may be a good one, and therefore deserving of accomplishment, yet through human casualties liable to defeat, the subjunctive is the proper mood for the expression of an unfulfilled purpose. Accordingly, no usage is more common or correct in Latin than *ut* fulfilling this function. But it is no less notorious that *ut* is found in almost every page of every Latin writer introducing a purpose that has passed into an actually accomplished fact. If the explanation of *ut* introducing an unfulfilled purpose be correct, then the usage of *ut* introducing an actually accomplished fact would appear not to be correct. No two notions could be conceived more contrary to each other, and in the expression of them by the same particle there seems to be a very striking contradiction. The author, when treating of the former of these two usages in his first treatise, was well aware of its apparent inconsistency with the latter, but not being able to give any explanation that seemed sufficient and satisfactory to his own mind, he deemed it the safer course to be silent. He had formerly discussed the subject with a distinguished metropolitan professor, and had come to the conclusion, if not the conviction, that the difficulty was inexplicable. The only written attempt to solve the problem which the author has seen, is the one published by Professor Madvig of Copenhagen, which he will quote before giving his own:—

"In some kinds of subordinate propositions the conjunctive is also used of a thing which the speaker asserts as existing, in order to show that it is not considered by itself, but as a subordinate member of another leading idea, *e. g.*, ita cucurri, ut vehementer sudurem. This last use of the conjunctive originated from the first and proper use, in consequence of the form being transferred from such subordinate propositions as express a simple conception (*e. g.*, final) to others which assert something actually existing (*e. g.*, consecutive propositions), because they agreed with the first in being conceived as depending on the leading proposition, and necessary to complete its signification. But while the subjunctive was so transferred and applied in some cases, in others, on the contrary, it was not so."—*Latin Grammar*, p. 296: Second Edition: translated by Woods: Parker, London

The latter part of this extract is not in itself very intelligible, and no part of it throws any light on the true nature of the subjunctive in general, or on *ut* introducing an actually accomplished fact, in particular. One thing, however, is quite clear, the doctrine of "dependence" is dragged in to do duty in dispelling the difficulty. That doctrine has already been discussed and disposed of in a preceding chapter. To introduce that doctrine in connexion with the point at issue, is to trifle with the subject, and to insult the human understanding. To show that dependence has nothing to do with the subject, that the subjunctive is entirely independent of dependence on a preceding clause, the following passages are adduced, two of which have been already adduced at an earlier stage of this argument. The one is the well-known line from Juvenal :—

Quis tulerit Gracchos de seditione querentes.—
*Sat.*, ii. 24.

Here there is no preceding clause on which *tulerit* can be supposed to depend. Hence the inevitable and irresistible inference follows, that the presence of the preceding clause does not produce the succeeding clause with its subjunctive, because its absence does not prevent the occurrence of the subjunctive in an independent clause. The excessive folly of any one in tolerating the Gracchi when complaining of mutiny, is ridiculed and repudiated by Juvenal, by means of the subjunctive, which is not subordinate to any preceding clause whatever. This idea is inherent in the subjunctive itself, and is altogether irrespective and independent of what goes before. Its affinity to the combination of *sunt qui* with the subjunctive, by which a writer repudiates the opinions or acts of others *as being either strange or wrong*, will also be apparent.

The other passage, which has been already alluded to, is from Virgil,—

> Quis possit fallere amantem?—*Æn.*, iv. 296.

Here the idea of being able to outwit a lover is repudiated as ridiculous. Virgil seems to entertain the same opinion on this point as Ovid himself, who represents Pyramus and Thisbe conversing through the chink of a wall, which though concealed from all others for many generations, was soon revealed to them:—

> Fissus erat tenui rima, quam duxerat olim,
> Quum fieret, paries domui communis utrique,
> Id vitium nulli per saecula longa notatum,
> *Quid non sentit* amor, primi sensistis amantes
> Et voci fecistis iter; tutaeque per illud
> Murmure blanditiae minimo transire solebant.—
> *Met.*, lib. iii., Pyr. and Thisb. 11.

The next passage is also taken from Virgil:—

> Mutemus clypeos, Danaumque insignia nobis
> Aptemus: dolus, an virtus, quis in hoste *requirat.*
> —*Æn.*, ii. 390.

This passage and the one just quoted prove that the Romans were familiar with the maxim,—all things are fair in love and war. The Trojans, beset before and behind in their beleaguered city, would naturally not scruple to avail themselves of any means of defence or offence. Virgil here represents them as assuming the armour of the Greeks, and by putting the words—

Dolus, an virtus, quis in hoste *requirat*

—in the mouth of one of their leaders, he repudiates, by means of the subjunctive, the imputation of any injustice in the act. This idea is inherent in the subjunctive itself, and is altogether irrespective and independent of any preceding clause.

There remains one other passage to be cited from Virgil, equally conclusive and decisive,—

Me tamen urit amor; quis enim modus *adsit* amori.
—*Ec.*, ii. 68.

The sentiment and the syntax are exactly similar to those of two other passages which have been given from the same poet. The idea of imposing any limit on love is repudiated as absurd and impossible, and by no other means or mood could this idea be expressed so appropriately as by the subjunctive, even though there is no preceding clause to exercise any influence on it.

This usage of the subjunctive being closely allied to all the other usages of that mood, both those which have been already given in this treatise, and those which still remain to be given in due course, is not confined to one or two poetical writers, but common to all the Roman writers, in prose as well as verse. The next illustrative instance is taken from Cicero,—

Ego te videre *noluerim?*—*Q. Fr.*, i. 3.

By the subjunctive here, altogether independent of the influence of any preceding clause, Cicero implies that the idea of his being unwilling to see his brother was both *absurd* and *unjust*.

The next and last illustrative instance of this independent usage of the subjunctive is taken from Terence:—

Quaeso, quid istuc consilii est,
Illius stultitia victa ex urbe rus tu habitatum *migres*.
—*Hec.*, iv. 2, 13.

By the employment of the independent subjunctive here, *migres*, Terence implies that the speaker Pamphilus both strongly disapproved of his mother's contemplated withdrawal into the country, and sought to dissuade her against it.

It has just been seen that these usages of the subjunctive are closely connected with those considered in the previous chapters. They are not less clearly connected with those clauses which contain a subjunctive with *ut* introducing a consequence,—the subject of the present chapter. This is no fancy, like the doctrine of "dependence," but a fact, as may clearly be seen from the following sentence from Cicero:—

> M. Egone ut te interpellem?—*Tusc.*, ii. 18.

Here the speaker repudiates the imputation of interrupting his interlocutor, as being contrary alike to his desire and his design. The subjunctive of itself implies as much. If, however, there could be any reasonable doubt, it would be removed by the immediately succeeding context:—

> Ne hoc quidem vellem: ita me ad credendum tua ducit oratio.

It will be observed, moreover, that there is no preceding clause to which *ut interpellem* can possibly be subordinate. Whatever Professor Madvig may have imagined, Cicero did not deem such a clause indispensable to the subjunctive; and on Latin at least, Cicero, without presumption, may be considered as good an authority as any modern German or even Dane.

The true theory of the subjunctive may be most clearly and conclusively demonstrated in connexion with the word *tantus*. First of all, let a sentence containing *tantus* with the indicative be selected for critical examination:—

> Frumentum *tanti* fuit, *quanti* iste aestimavit.—Cic., *Ver.*, 3, 84, 194.

If ever, with any propriety or truth, it could be

said that one clause was "dependent on another, or the complement" of another, it might be said so of *quanti iste aestimavit*, in reference to frumentum tanti fuit. But, nevertheless, the "dependent" clause, or "complement," as it is called, contains an indicative—quanti *aestimavit*—contrary to the common doctrine. On the other hand, six sentences in succession, quoted above, contained independent clauses with the subjunctive, contrary to the conventional rule of grammarians. The only rule known to the Romans was, that the syntax should be subordinate to the sense, and that the sense should determine the form of the sentence. In the sentence just quoted, Cicero employed the indicative in both clauses, because he desired and designed *to state two ordinary facts of co-ordinate importance*.

Before adducing illustrative instances of "tantus" with the subjunctive, in contradistinction to its usage with the indicative, it will be necessary to advert to a fact in connexion with this word, which the author has never seen noted anywhere, and which really contains the germ of the true theory of the subjunctive. It is certainly a somewhat striking fact, that while the primary and proper meaning of "tantus" is *so great*, its derivative adverb "tantum," should mean *only, so little*. In "tantus," *so great*, and "tantum," *so little*, is found a striking illustration of the maxim—extremes meet. "Tantus" either meaning *so much* or *so little*, is appropriately followed by the subjunctive, for *the true theory of this mood is, that it is employed to express what is extraordinary or exceptional, either what rises above or what falls below the ordinary standard.*

Now that this is shown to be the true function of the subjunctive, nothing can be more natural, though before it seemed an anomaly, for *which no sufficient or satisfactory account could be given,* than *that the subjunctive should express an actually accomplished result* introduced by *ut,* since the result is an extraordinary or exceptional result, and since it has also been shown that the true function of the indicative is to express an *ordinary* fact, without condition, qualification, or reserve. Hitherto it has been believed by British and Continental scholars, that the indicative is the mood of fact, and the subjunctive the mood of conception. There can be no doubt that there is a small amount of truth in this opinion, and that this theory deserves more respect than the theory of the "essential part;" or Grotefend and Forbiger's theory of the "conditional;" or the theory of the "predicate;" but though not so great a delusion as any of these, it is, nevertheless, a delusion. The late Professor Zumpt, of the University, and Member of the Royal Academy, Berlin, who, if not the first to propound the theory of the "essential part," adopted it, adopted also, if he was not the first to propound it, the theory that "the indicative is the mood of fact," and "the subjunctive is the mood of conception." He says,—

"The subjunctive is used in general, when a proposition is stated *not as a fact, but as a conception of the mind.*—2d edition, p. 376, by Schmitz.

Such a generalization could only have been the result of a very partial examination and study of the Latin language. The *essential characteristic and condition* of each mood has escaped the observation of Professor Zumpt altogether. The difference between the two moods is not that *fact* is peculiar to the one, and *conception* to the other, but that *one class of facts is stated by the one, and another class of facts by the other.* The following usages of the subjunctive prove that the statement of fact belongs to it as well as to the indicative:—

Tranquillis rebus, fama Gallici belli pro tumultu valuit, *ut* dictatorem dici *placeret.*—Livy, lib. viii. 17.

Here, the *fact* of a resolution being passed for the appointment of a dictator, is stated by the *subjunctive*, without condition, qualification, or reserve.

Accidit, *ut* una nocte omnes Hermae, qui in oppido erant Athenis, *dejicerentur.*—Nep., *Alcib.*, 3.

Here *ut* preceded by *accidit* (it happened) introduces a fact expressed emphatically by the subjunctive, as in the preceding sentence, without qualification, condition, or reserve. The Athenians, seeing with their own eyes, had the best evidence for saying that the statues of Hermes had been thrown down. Men may disbelieve their ears, but never their eyes.

Sunt qui suum se negotium agere *dicant,* ne facere cuiquam videantur injuriam.—Cic., *Off.*, i. 29.

Cicero as much states a fact by the subjunctive *dicant*, as he does by the indicative *sunt*, and with far greater emphasis, for he wrote the sentence, not to tell his readers that certain men *existed*, but that they *said* what he condemned. These men, like Cain, affected not to be their brothers' keepers.

*Quum* id *nuntiatum esset* Cæsari, eos per provinciam nostram iter facere conari, maturat ab urbe proficisci et quam maximis potest itineribus in Galliam ulteriorem contendit et ad Genevam pervenit.—Cæs., *De Bel. Gal.*, lib. i. 7.

What is stated by the subjunctive *nuntiatum esset* must be a fact, otherwise the whole Gallic war was a fiction, or, as the Germans phrase it, a myth. Not only was it a fact, but it was the fountain whence all the other facts flowed, contained in the Commentaries. It was no less a *fact* that intelligence of civil and military disturbances in Gaul was received by Cæsar, than it is a fact within our own remembrance, that similar intelligence relative to India was received by the British Government, when Sir Charles Napier was despatched on his last errand to that country.

> *Irae* Thyesten exitio gravi
> Stravere, et altis urbibus ultimae
> Stetere causae, cur *perirent*
> Funditus imprimeretque muris
> Hostile aratrum exercitus insolens.
> —Hor., lib. i., *Car.* xvi.

Whether Troy had a historical existence or no,

whether the *anger* of the Greeks was the cause of its fall, may or may not be a fact, but there can be no doubt that the capture and conflagration of Carthage were *facts — perirent —* and that the anger of the Romans was the cause, as may be inferred by one, out of many indications of the national temper,— the well-known peroration of Cato:—

Caeterum censeo, Patres Conscripti, Carthaginem delendam.

Paucis ante diebus quam Syracusae *caperentur,* Otacilius in Africam transmisit.—Liv., xxv. 31.

There can be no doubt that the capture of Syracuse was a historical *fact,* and that fact is most appropriately expressed by the subjunctive.

These six sentences in succession exhibit different, but not diverse, usages of the subjunctive, for a unity in expressing a *fact* underlies them all. The consideration which guided the Romans in the choice of their mood was the character of the deed to be described. If the character of the deed was an ordinary one, they employed the indicative, if it was an extraordinary or exceptional one, they employed the subjunctive. In like manner, *conception belongs to the indicative as well as to the subjunctive, as has already been seen in a previous part of the work. If the conception introduced by* si *implies probability, the indicative is employed; if, on the other hand, improbability or impossibility is implied, the subjunctive is employed.* Such is the *logical consistency* which the Latin language uniformly exhibits.

Having now proved that the expression of a fact belongs to the subjunctive as well as to the indicative, and that the expression of a conception belongs to the indicative as well as to the subjunctive, and that it is only the character of the conception or fact which constitutes the true criterion by which the mood is determined, it is now time to show by illustrative examples under what circumstances the Romans employed the subjunctive to state a fact.

As has been already remarked, the true theory of the subjunctive is most concisely and correctly exhibited in connexion with the word *tantus*. The remarkable circumstance that it bears the meaning of "so little," as well as "so great," finds its explanation in the fact that each meaning is only *the expression of an extreme*, whatever rises above or falls below an ordinary standard. Each extreme meets by finding a common expression in the subjunctive.

The following are instances of *tantus*, "so excessively small," requiring a subjunctive:—

Ceterarum provinciarum vectigalia *tanta* sunt, ut iis ad ipsas tutandas provincias vix contenti esse *possimus*. The revenues of the other dependencies are so excessively small, that we can scarcely be satisfied with them for the protection of the dependencies themselves. —Cic., *Man*. vi. 14.

Si bellum *tantum* erit, *ut* vos aut successores sustinere possint. If the war shall be on so small a scale, that you or your successors may be able to support it.—*Coel*. in l. c., *Fam*., 8, 10.

Praesidii *tantum* est, *ut* ne murus quidem cingi possit, neque quisquam egredi extra munitiones audeat. They have not force enough to man the wall, or for any one to venture to go out of the fortifications.—Cæs., *De Bel. Gal.*, vi. 35.

*Tantum* navium repperit *ut* anguste xv. millia legionariorum militum transportare *possent*. He found so few vessels that they were hardly capable of conveying across fifteen thousand regular troops.— Cæs., *B. C.*, iii. 2.

Nec sidera *tanta* debent existimari, *quanta* cernuntur. Nor is it right to deem the stars so small, as they seem to be.—Pliny.

Nor is it with *tantus*, "excessively little," alone, that this usage of the subjunctive is found. There are other forms of expression, if not the same, yet similar in force, which show that the idea was quite familiar to the Roman mind, and the one they had formed of the subjunctive, however foreign to the fancies of modern grammarians.

Oratio Appii *ad id modo* valuit, *ut* tempus rogationum jubendarum *proferretur*. The speech of Appius had only this effect, that the time for passing the bills was deferred.—Livy, vi. 42.

Quum intercedendo tribuni *nihil aliud*, quam *ut differrent* comitia valuissent, duo patricii consules creati sunt. The tribunes having effected nothing else by their protest, than the postponement of the election, two consuls of Patrician rank were appointed.— Livy, vii. 17.

The connexion between the conception of *excessive* smallness in objects or results, and excessive smallness in the number of persons or things, distinguished for something or other *extraordinary*, is clear and certain. Each idea is an extreme. Accordingly, the Romans, in consistency with the genius of their language, expressed each extreme by employing the subjunctive. Perhaps the best illustration of this cognate usage of the subjunctive that the Latin language can furnish is to be found in connexion with the Phoenix, to which a reference has already been made. It is notorious that the ancients believed that one, and only one Phoenix existed at the same time. Of it Ovid says:—

    Et vivax Phoenix, *unica* semper avis.
                  —*Am.*, lib. ii., *El.* vi.

As no number can be smaller than one, so no description can be more *exclusive, extreme*, or *extraordinary* than that expressed by *unicus*. It is applied properly by Livy to Archimedes:—

Et habuisset, tanto impetu coepta, res fortunam, nisi *unus* homo Syracusis ea tempestate fuisset. Archimedes is erat, *unicus* spectator coeli siderumque. —Livy, lib. xxiv. 34.

With equal propriety Livy employs *unicus* to describe an act, to which Roman history could present no parallel. Speaking of Attalus, he says:—

    Unicam praestitit fidem.—xxxiii. 21.

Such, then, being the extraordinary characteristics of the Phoenix, no description of it, however elaborate, could be accurate or adequate, unless made by the employment of the most powerful and exquisite organ of human expression, the subjunctive mood. Hence, Ovid, in the very first line of a description which combines all these conditions, employs the subjunctive:—

*Una est* quae *reparet*, seque ipsa *reseminet*, ales;
Assyrii Phoenica vocant: non fruge, nec herbis,
Sed turis lacrimis, et succo vivit amomi.
—*Met.* xv. 391.

According to Dr Carson, Dr Parr, and their faithful followers, the relative clause *quae reparet*, contains the predicate of the sentence, by their rule, whose condition is, "The precise subjects to which the author alludes must be *unknown* to him, and *undefined*." —*Qui, Quae, Quod,* p. 6. In the first line of the extract, it will be observed, Ovid describes from *knowledge* accurately acquired the extraordinary conditions of existence attributed to a certain bird; in the very next line he expressly *names it.* Of course there was only one such bird on the face of the earth. And yet Dr Carson, with Dr Parr's sanction, wrote, "The subject must be unknown to the author, and undefined." But the author begs pardon for alluding again, even though casually, to a doctrine so utterly erroneous. The Phoenix, whose properties Ovid so appropriately expresses by the subjunctive, remarkable for the extraordinary conditions of its existence, was no less remarkable for the duration of its existence. There were many animals known to the ancients remarkable for their longevity, but the Phoenix was the most remarkable of all. Hesiod has a fragment beginning thus:—

Ἐννέα τοι ζώει γενεὰς λακέρυζα κορώνη—

which Ausonius translates:—

Ter binos, deciesque novem super exit in annos
Justa senescentum quos implet vita virorum,
Ilos novies superat vivendo garrula cornix:
Et quater egreditur cornicis secula cervus.
Alipedem cervum ter vincit corvus: et illum
Multiplicat novies *Phoenix*, reparabilis ales.
—*Eid.* xviii.

Nepos, in his life of Aristides, furnishes a usage of *unus*, precisely parallel to the usage furnished by Ovid. *Unus* there introduces a fact, so extraordinary, that the biographer could produce no precedent or parallel. The description of such a fact could, of course, only be made by means of the subjunctive mood.

Quamquam enim adeo excellebat Aristides abstinentia, *ut unus post hominum memoriam*, quod quidem nos audiverimus, cognomine justus *appellatus sit*: tamen, a Themistocle collabefactus, testula illa exilio decem annorum mulctatus est. For, although Aristides was so conspicuous for his self-control, that he alone, within the remembrance of men, as far, at least, as we have heard, was styled by surname the Just, yet, having been supplanted by Themistocles, he, by means of the notorious process of ostracism, was sentenced to banishment for ten years.—*Aris.* i.

Livy furnishes another usage, which, though not exactly the same as that just given, is very similar. The fact was not without a precedent, indeed; but the long period of seven hundred years only furnished two others. Such a fact was sufficiently extraordinary to account for the subjunctive mood. The language which Livy employs shows how much he was impressed by the fact:—

Mitigandum ferocem populum armorum desuetudine ratus, Janum ad infimum Argiletum, indicem pacis bellique, fecit: apertus, ut in armis esse civitatem; clausus, pacatos circa omnes populos, significaret. Bis deinde post Numae regnum clausus fuit: semel T. Manlio consule, post Punicum primum perfectum bellum: iterum, quod nostrae aetati *dii dederunt ut videremus*, post bellum Actiacum ab imperatore Cæsare Augusto, pace terra marique parta. Numa, believing that a warlike people could be humanized by the discontinuance of hostilities, erected a temple to Janus at the bottom of the street, Argiletum, as an index of peace and war. Twice afterwards, subsequent to the reign of Numa, was it shut; once in the consulship of T. Manlius, after the termination of the first Punic war; a second time, a privilege which the gods allowed our age to see after the battle of

Actium, by the Emperor Cæsar Augustus, when he had secured peace by land and by sea.—Lib. i. 19.

The ascription of the closing of the temple of Janus to the direct intervention of the gods by Livy, and the unusualness of the combination *dederunt ut*, alike attest the importance and extraordinary nature of the fact. The sentiment and syntax of Livy are equally striking and significant.

There is another passage from Livy, which, though it does not contain the word *unus*, contains the statement of a fact, without a precedent, expressed, of course, by means of the subjunctive.

Approbantibus cunctis, diem Manlio dicunt. Quod ubi factum est, primo commota est plebs, utique post quam sordidatum reum viderunt, nec cum eo non modo patrum quemquam sed ne cognatos quidem aut adfinis, postremo ne frates quidem Aulum et Titum Manlium, *quod ad eum diem nunquam usu venisset, ut* in tanto discrimine, non et proximi, vestem *mutarent:* Appio Claudio in vincla ducto, C. Claudium inimicum Claudiamque omnem gentem sordidatum fuisse. Amid universal assent, they fixed a day for the impeachment of Manlius. And when this had taken place, at first the commons were greatly affected, especially after that they beheld the culprit clad in mean attire, unaccompanied not only by none of the patricians, but not even by one of his blood or marriage relations; at last, when they saw not even his brothers, Aulus and Titus Manlius, his own nearest kindred, change their dress in a crisis so terrible, *a circumstance which never had happened before;* when Appius Claudius had been led to prison, Caius Claudius, though his private enemy, and the entire Claudian clan, had clad themselves in mean attire.—Livy, vi. 20.

The next illustrative instance of *ut* with the subjunctive, also from Livy, introduces a fact, which, if not altogether so remarkable for rarity as the preceding one, is almost as much so, and resembles it sufficiently to require the appropriate mood:—

Additus triumpho *honos,* ut statuae equestres eis, *rara* illa aetate *res,* in foro *ponerentur.* Besides the triumph, they had the additional distinction accorded them, of getting equestrian effigies erected in the forum, a thing which seldom happened in that age. —Lib. vi. 13.

The next illustrative instance of *ut* with the subjunctive, from Cæsar, introduces the mention of a mode of punishment, exceptional and excessive to an extreme degree, and one, therefore, which would not be often executed:—

Moribus suis Orgetorigem ex vinculis causam dicere coegerunt: damnatum poenam sequi oportebat *ut igni* cremaretur. The punishment consequent on conviction was that he should be consumed by fire.—*De Bel. Gal.*, lib. i. 4.

Readers of Roman history will remember, that when Pompey applied for a triumph to the senate, Sylla especially objected, on the ground that he had never been consul, and that he was only twenty-four years of age.

## THE FUNCTION OF UT. 139

The next extract exhibits another Roman, as consul, at the earlier age of twenty-three. Livy, of course, gives expression to an event so extraordinary by the employment of the subjunctive:—

Ea aetate consulatum adeptus sum, *ut potuerim, tres* et *viginti* annos natus, consul patribus quoque ferox, non solum plebi. I attained the consulship at such an age, that when only twenty-three years old, I proved a stern consul to the patricians as well as to the commons.—Livy, vii. 40.

The next extract presents a combination of circumstances equally extraordinary with any hitherto enumerated. The parts peculiar to the respective actors on the scene are exchanged. Men perform the part of women, women perform the part of men. Both parts are represented by the subjunctive:—

Tum matronae ad Veturiam, matrem Coriolani, Volumniamque uxorem frequentes coeunt. Id publicum consilium, an muliebris timor fuerit, parum invenio. Pervicere certe *ut* et Veturia magno natu mulier, et Volumnia, duos parvos ex Marcio ferens filios, secum in castra hostium irent; et, quam armis viri defendere urbem *non possent*, mulieres precibus lacrymisque *defenderent*.

At that time the Roman dames in great crowds repair to Veturia, the mother of Coriolanus. Whether that act was undertaken at the instance of the government or prompted by the fear of women, I have not been able to ascertain. They assuredly prevailed on Veturia, a woman far advanced in years, and Volumnia, bearing her two little sons by Marcius, to repair with them to the camp of the enemy; and women by prayers and tears succeeded in protecting that city, which men had been unable to protect by the arts of war.—Livy, ii. 40.

The two last illustrative instances of an *extreme in smallness*, introduced by *ut* with the subjunctive, are taken from Livy and Nepos. The coincidence in circumstance and construction is complete, and furnishes the clearest evidence of what was the ruling idea associated by the Romans with the subjunctive. The first of the two passages is from Livy:—

P. Valerius, omnium consensu princeps belli pacisque artibus, anno post, Agrippa Menenio, P. Postumio consulibus, moritur; gloria ingenti, copiis familiaribus *adeo exiguis*, ut funeri sumptus deesset; de publico est datus.

P. Valerius, by universal assent, the foremost man in the pursuits of peace and war, in the year afterwards, during the consulship of Agrippa Menenius and P. Postumius, dies with great renown, but with private property so *extremely* small, that means to defray his funeral expenses were wanting. He was buried at the expense of the state.—ii. 17.

The other passage, from Nepos, is,—

Hic qua fuerit abstinentia, nullum est certius indicium, quam quod, quum tantis rebus praefuisset, in tanta paupertate discessit, *ut*, qui efferretur, vix reliqueret.

Of what moderation the subject of our biography was, there is no surer proof, than the fact, although he presided over the conduct of the most important affairs, that he died in such poverty that he scarcely left wherewith he might be buried.—*Aris.*, iii.

It is now time to adduce in demonstration and illustration instances of the other extreme expressed by the subjunctive—the *extreme of greatness, of very various kinds*. In the following extract from Cæsar, the peculiar idea is expressed with all the emphasis of which language is capable:—

Dum paucos dies ad Vesontionem rei frumentariae commeatusque causa moratur, ex percontatione nostrorum vocibusque Gallorum ac mercatorum, qui ingenti magnitudine corporum Germanos, incredibili virtute atque exercitatione in armis esse, praedicabant, saepenumero sese cum his congressos ne vultum quidem atque aciem oculorum ferre potuisse, tantus subito timor omnem exercitum occupavit, *ut non mediocriter* omnium mentes animosque *perturbaret*.

While he stays a few days in the vicinity of Besançon, for the sake of procuring corn and other provisions, in consequence of the interrogations of our men, and the conversation of the Gauls and merchants, who openly affirmed that the Germans were men of immense stature, of marvellous valour and experience in the art of war, that having repeatedly encountered them in the field, they could not so much as endure the expression of their countenance, and the glance of their eye; such fear suddenly seized the whole army, that it disconcerted to an *extraordinary* degree their understandings and feelings.—*Bel. Gal.*, lib. i. 39.

The expression *non mediocriter*, indicates clearly and conclusively enough the conception Cæsar had formed of the subjunctive. That conception, as will be seen from the illustrative examples already adduced, was one held in common with his countrymen. One or two other passages may be cited from Cæsar combining the same conditions and pointing to the same conclusions:—

Flumen est Arar, quod per fines Aeduorum et Sequanorum in Rhodanum influit, *incredibili* lenitate, ita *ut* oculis in utram partem fluat judicari non *possit*.

The Saone is a river which flows through the territories of the Sequani and Aedui into the Rhone, with such *extraordinary* smoothness, that it cannot be determined by the eye in what direction it flows.—*Bel. Gal.*, i. 12.

Many, if not most rivers, the Rhone among the number, run with rapid rush into the sea. Cæsar, who was familiar with such, was naturally struck with the extreme contrast presented by the course of the Saone, and expressed himself with regard to it in the strong language employed above.

The second passage is as follows:—

Gallis magno ad pugnam impedimento quod pluribus eorum scutis uno ictu pilorum transfixis et colligatis, quum ferrum se inflexisset, neque evellere neque sinistra impedita satis commode pugnare poterant, multi *ut* diu jactato brachio *praeoptarent* scutum manu emittere et nudo corpore pugnare.

It proved a great obstruction to the Gauls in fight,

the fact that several of their shields having been pierced through and bound together by a single throw of darts, when once the point of the missile had bent itself, they were neither able to pluck it out, nor, from the consequent entanglement of their left hand, could they maintain the combat with sufficient ease, so that many, after tossing and tugging their arm for a long time, preferred throwing away their shield and fighting with their bodies exposed.—*Bel. Gal.*, i. 25.

This mode of fighting was *strange*, if *not wrong*. The usage of the subjunctive in describing it is closely and clearly connected with the primary and proper usage of the subjunctive in reported speech, whereby a writer implied that he was not responsible for the sentiments of another, and might repudiate them as strange or wrong. This usage of the subjunctive is also closely and clearly connected with the usage of the subjunctive in such clauses as *sunt qui dicant*, by which a class of individuals are indicated who say strange or wrong things. So closely connected and consistent with each other are all the usages of the subjunctive, whatever philologists hitherto may have believed.

The next illustrative instance, from Nepos, containing the essential element of excess, in the shape of extreme valour, is as follows:—

In quo proelio tanto plus virtute valuerunt Athenienses, *ut decemplicem numerum hostium profligarent;* adeoque perterruerunt *ut* Persae non castra, sed naves *peterent*.

In this battle the Athenians were so far superior in valour, that of the enemy they routed ten times their number; and to such an extent did they terrify the Persians, that they fled not to their camp, but to their ships.—*Mil.*, 5.

Despite the great numerical disproportion between the Greeks and the Persians, the former won a most signal victory over the latter. On the one side there was an excessively small force, on the other side there was an excessively large force. This peculiar combination of circumstances combines all the conditions requisite for the constitution of a striking extreme.

The next illustrative instance is equally striking in its own way. Whatever exceeds the experience of ordinary observation, whatever exceeds the limits of a moderate estimate, any deviation from the golden mean, *an addition to an amount already sufficient*, finds its fitting expression by means of the subjunctive. Though Livy had been desirous to demonstrate directly the true theory of the subjunctive, he could not have done it more clearly and conclusively than he has done by his description of the position of affairs at Rome in a certain memorable year of its history:—

Eodem anno, quum *satis per se ipsum* Samnitium bellum et defectio repens Latinorum, auctoresque defectionis Tarentini sollicitos haberent patris, *accessit ut*, et Vestinus populus Samnitibus sese conjungeret.

In the same year, when the war with the Samnites, enough in itself, and the sudden revolt of the Lucanians, and the people of Tarentum, who were its mitigators, were keeping the senators in a state of anxiety, this state of affairs was aggravated by the union of the Vestini with the Samnites.—viii. 29.

The golden mean—*satis per se*—followed by the crowning extreme—*accessit ut et Vestinus populus sese Samnitibus conjungeret*—is singularly striking and significant.

That Livy desired and designed to represent with all the emphasis peculiar to the Latin language an extraordinary circumstance to crown others, in the combination—*accessit ut et conjungeret*—is proved by the following passage from another part of his great work:—

Nam etiam illud accedit, ne tam clara pugna in eum annum transferri posset, *quod* imbelle triennium ferme pestilentia, inopiaque frugum, circa A. Cornelium consulem *fuit*.

For this is an additional proof that so celebrated a battle could not be transferred to that year, the fact that a period of three years, about the time that A. Cornelius was consul, was almost free from war in consequence of an epidemic and scarcity of provisions. —Lib. iv. 20.

Here the word *accedit*, the same as in the preceding passage, when followed by *quod*, introduces simply an additional fact, and accordingly requires the indicative. This may be inferred from a consideration of the clause itself. In another part, however, of the same book, Livy does not leave his reader to draw the inference indirectly, but directly intimates in words, that the fact introduced by *quod* was not one of significant import.

Insigni magnis rebus, anno additur, *nihil tum ad rem Romanam pertinere visum,* quod Carthaginienses, tanti hostes futuri, tum primum per seditiones Siculorum ad partis alterius auxilium in Siciliam exercitum trajecere.

To the history of this year, remarkable for important events, is added the fact, which appeared not at all to affect the Roman state at that time, that the Carthaginians destined to prove so formidable foes, in consequence of the revolt of its states, transported an army into Sicily to aid the other side.—Lib. iv. 29.

Livy here expressly states that the fact introduced by *quod* with the indicative—quod Carthaginienses in Siciliam exercitum trajecere—seemed of little importance, and merely introduces it incidentally in closing the history of a year remarkable (*insigni*) for events, whose greater importance he indicates by the greater space he devotes to their description.

Two other passages from Livy may be cited containing *accedo;* one with it followed by the indicative, another with it followed by the subjunctive. The difference of meaning is indicated by the difference of mood in a manner not to be mistaken. The first passage is,—

Auguriis certe *tantus honos accessit,* ut nihil belli domique postea, nisi auspicato, *gereretur:* concilia populi, exercitus vocati, summa rerum, ubi aves non admisissent, dirimerentur.

So great consideration accrued to divination, and the college of soothsayers, that nothing afterwards, during peace or war, was transacted without consulting the omens; the assemblies of the people, the summoning of armies, the most important concerns of the state, were postponed whenever the birds had not given their sanction.—i. 36.

The consideration now accorded to the college of soothsayers, and never accorded before, not only the highest the Romans could bestow, but than which a higher it is impossible to conceive, is expressed by *accessit ut* with the *subjunctive*. On the other hand, the circumstance introduced by *accessit* with *quod* and the indicative in the following passage is of a very different character:—

Ceterum id quoque ad gloriam *accessit*, quod cum illo, simul justa ac legitima regna occiderunt.

But that also contributes to his renown, the fact that fair and constitutional government perished at the same time with him.—Liv., i. 48.

The scholar will remember, without being reminded, that these words refer to the great sovereign and statesman Servius Tullius, who conceived and completed a series of constitutional reforms such as no Roman king either achieved or attempted. The historian, after recounting the chief acts of his reign, those only with which he was directly concerned, those only which could determine his character as an administrator, those only for which he could strictly claim credit, alludes to a circumstance, which, as it was in no way connected with him, as over it he had no control, reflecting strongly on the character of his successor, only indirectly, by way of contrast, could be construed as a contribution to his fame. This incidental fact—accessit quod legitima regna cum eo occiderunt—is of course expressed by the indicative. The contrast between the two usages of *accessit* in these two extracts, disposes completely of the doctrine of dependence, to say nothing of what has already been said about and against it in a preceding chapter of this work. It is quite clear that the clause—quod regna cum eo occiderunt—is dependent on *accessit*, that the former clause is the complement of the latter, that "it is an essential part of the entire statement,"—rules which grammarians say require the subjunctive, and yet after all the indicative—occiderunt—is employed. The Romans, to whom these rules were unknown, who saw no virtue in arbitrary combinations of words apart from their sense, allowed the sense only to regulate the syntax of a sentence.

The next three illustrative instances of an extraordinary event introduced by *ut* with the subjunctive are so certain and conspicuous as not to need any accompanying comment.

His atrocioribusque, credo, aliis, quae praesens rerum indignitas haudquaquam relatu scriptoribus facilia, subjecit, memoratis, incensam multitudinem *perpulit, ut imperium regi abrogaret*, exulesque case juberet L. Tarquinium cum conjuge ac liberis.

By recounting these and other deeds, I believe,

more shameful still, which the atrocity of the present outrage suggested, but by no means easy for the historian to narrate, he *compelled* the exasperated populace *to strip* king Tarquin of *his crown*, and to pass a decree that he, with his wife and children, should go into banishment.—Livy, lib. i. 59.

Tunc *adeo* fracti simul cum corpore sunt spiritus illi feroces, *ut*, qui nihil ante ratus esset minus regium, quam sacris dedere animum, repente omnibus magnis parvisque superstitionibus obnoxius *degeret* religionibusque etiam populum *impleret*.

To such a degree was that dauntless spirit broken along with his body, that he who had deemed previously nothing less becoming a king, than to bestow his attention on holy rites, all of a *sudden* became a prey to small as well as great superstitions, and imbued the people also with religious scruples.—Livy, i. 31.

Nullo unquam proelio fugae minus, nec plus caedis fuisset, ni obstinatos mori Tuscos non texisset: ita *ut victores*, priusquam victi, pugnandi finem *facerent*.

In no battle was there ever less flight, and in none would there have been more slaughter, had not night interposed to protect the Tuscans determined to die; so that the conquerors, sooner than the conquered, left the field.—Livy, ix. 32.

Livy, who has furnished already so many illustrative examples of *extremes* introduced by *ut* with the subjunctive, shall also furnish the two last to be given here, one of an extreme rising far above an ordinary standard, another of an extreme falling far below an ordinary standard. One chapter contains both, with but a few words between, both being put by the historian into the mouth of the same speaker, —so familiar to the Roman mind was the fixed idea which they had formed of the function of the subjunctive. The first instance is an extreme rising far above the ordinary standard.

*Quo ultra* iram violentiamque ejus excessuram fuisse, quam *ut necaret verberaretque?*

To what more extreme pitch could his anger and intemperate conduct have proceeded, than to inflict the punishment of stripes and death?—Lib. viii. 33.

The second illustrative instance falling far below an ordinary standard, is:—

Nam populi quidem, penes quem potestas omnium rerum esset, ne iram quidem unquam atrociorem in eos fuisse, qui temeritate atque inscitia exercitus amisissent, quam *ut pecunia* eos *multaret*.

For not even the anger of the people, in whom supreme powers in all matters was vested, ever vented itself in greater severity against those who by their rashness and ignorance had sacrificed the armies of the state, than in imposing on them a pecuniary fine.—*Id.*

Confirmation of these views in the form of direct demonstration, comes from all parts of Latin literature. As it has been seen above, that *accedit* with *quod* and the *indicative*, introduces an *ordinary* fact, while *accedit* with *ut* and the *subjunctive* introduce an *extraordinary* fact, so *verisimile* with the accusative and *infinitive* introduce what is *probable*, while *verisimile* with *ut* and the subjunctive, on the other hand, introduce what is *improbable.* Cicero in one and the same speech proves these two positions:—

Verisimile est, istam rem ad Chrysogonum *detulisse.*—*Rosc.* 106.

Verisimile *non* est, *ut* Chrysogonus horum literas *adamavit.*—*Id.* 121.

Still further, there is a remarkable passage in Cicero, where, with *ut* and the *subjunctive,* he states opinions held by others, which reason pronounces to be *strange,* and conscience condemns as *wrong,* in opposition to his own opinion, which the majority of men consider both *reasonable* and *right.*

Quorum ea *sententia* est, *ut virtus per se ipsa nihil valeat,* omneque, *honestum* et *laudabile,* id *cassum quiddam* et inani vocis sono decoratum esse *dicant.*—*Tusc.,* v. 41.

So that the usage of the subjunctive in—Ea *sententia* est, ut virtus per se nil valeat — is precisely of the same import as the subjunctive in—Sunt qui dicant, *i.e.* there are those who say what is strange or wrong: and in — Socrates accusatus est quod *corrumperet* juventutem,—where the writer reports the sentiment of others, for which he is not responsible, and therefore repudiates.

The idea of excess either in the direction of what is wrong or strange, is thus so closely connected with the subjunctive mood, and consequently all the usages of this mood are consistent in the possession of a common characteristic.

Hitherto, in the illustrative instances of *ut* with the subjunctive introducing an extraordinary fact or circumstance, *ut* has been usually, if not uniformly, preceded by one or other of these intensives,—*tam, tantus, adeo*. Of course, the idea inherent in the subjunctive is entirely independent of the conventional syntactical combinations formed by these intensive words, since this mood is found without them, as well as with them. Their presence does not produce the subjunctive, because their absence does not prevent the occurrence of that mood. *Tam, tantus, adeo*, are the occasional concomitants of the subjunctive, but they are never the essential cause.

There is another very common syntactical combination in Latin, *accidit ut, forte evenit ut, fors ita tulit ut*, without any of the intensives just disposed of, but followed by the subjunctive. It will be found in this as well as in the preceding combinations, that *ut* introduces some thing or other extraordinary. The first passage cited in proof of this will be the well-known line of Horace:—

> Qui fit, Maecenas, *ut* nemo, quam sibi sortem
> Seu ratio dederit seu fors objecerit, illa
> Contentus *vivat*, laudet diversa sequentes?

How comes it to pass, Maecenas, that no one lives satisfied with the lot, which either choice may have given him, or chance thrown in his way, but deems those blessed who follow pursuits different from his own?—*Sat.*, lib. i. 1.

That the result expressed by *ut nemo contentus vivat* seemed to Horace a strange one, and made a deep impression on his mind, is proved by the fact, that the very first words of his first satire—*qui fit*—contain the question demanding an explanation of the enigma. The entire satire was desired and designed to be an answer.

The next passage, combining the same condition and pointing to the same conclusion, as that one from Horace, is taken from Nepos. It has already been quoted, but for a different purpose. It was formerly cited to prove that the subjunctive expressed a fact, as well as the indicative. It is now cited to show that the proper and peculiar function of the subjunctive is to express an extraordinary or exceptional fact. To the Athenians, the fact, which is here described, appeared both strange and ominous, for Nepos subsequently adds:—

Hoc quum appareret non sine magna multorum consensione esse factum, quod non ad privatam, sed ad publicam rem pertineret, *magnus multitudini timor est injectus, ne qua repentina vis in civitate exsisteret, quae libertatem populi opprimeret.*

The overthrow of the statues of Hermes seemed to foreshadow the overthrow of freedom, of which the Athenians were peculiarly jealous.

In the three last illustrative instances of *ut* with the subjunctive that remain to be adduced, it will be observed that an *extraordinary coincidence* with another preceding fact, is introduced by that mood:—

Hic non solum proximo regi dissimilis, sed ferocior etiam Romulo fuit: tum aetas viresque, tum avita quoque gloria animum stimulabat. Senescere igitur civitatem otio ratus, *undique materiam excitandi belli quaerebat.* Forte evenit, *ut agrestes Romani ex Albano agro, Albani ex agro Romano, praedas invicem agerent.* Imperitabat tum C. Cluilius Albae: utrimque legati fere sub idem tempus, ad res repetendas missi. Tullus praeceperat suis, ne quid prius, quam mandata agerent: satis sciebat, negaturum Albanum: *ita pie bellum indici posse.*—Livy, i. 22.

Here the historian states that Tullus was on the outlook for an outbreak of hostilities, and at the very time it so happened that Roman rustics were driving booty from the Alban territory, and Albans again in turn were doing the same in the Roman territory. The striking coincidence is accordingly appropriately marked by the employment of the subjunctive,— Forte evenit, ut Romani et Albani praedas *invicem agerent.*

The coincidence in the two other cases is still more extraordinary,—

L. Genucio consuli ea provincia sorte evenit. In expectatione civitas erat, quod primus ille de plebe consul bellum suis auspiciis gesturus esset: *perinde ut eviniret res, ita communicatos honores prospere aut secus consulto habitura.* Forte ita *tulit casus, ut* Genucius, ad hostes magno conatu profectus, in insidias *prae-*

*cipitaretur;* legionibusque necopinato pavore fusis consul circumventus ab insciis, quem interfecissent, occideretur.—Livy, vii. 6.

The circumstances under which Genucius assumed the command as consul were quite peculiar. He was the first of the plebeians who had taken the auspices, a privilege hitherto peculiar to the patricians. The state, in the meantime in suspense, considered the honour bestowed for good or ill (prospere aut secus consulto) precisely according to the issue of the campaign (perinde ac res eveniret). It so happened that Genucius was drawn into an ambuscade and slain, and thus by a way the most decisive of all others determined the question at issue.

The coincidence in the last case of all is equally extraordinary.

L. Annius of Setia, one of the Latin leaders, made a proposal to imperial Rome, without precedent or parallel for audacity and arrogance,—Consulem alterum Roma, alterum ex Latio creari oportet: senatus partem aequam ex utraque gente esse: unum populum, unam rempublicam fieri.

To this Livy says,—

Forte ita *accedit, ut parem ferociae hujus* et Romani consulem T. Manlium *haberent:* qui adeo non tenuit iram, ut si tanta dementia Patres conscriptos cepisset, ut ab Setino homine leges acciperent, gladio cinctum in senatum se esse venturum, palam diceret, et quemcunque in curia Latinum vidisset, sua manu interempturum.

It so happened by chance that the Romans also had a match for the audacity of this man in the consul, T. Manlius, who so far from restraining his indignation, openly declared that if such infatuation should take possession of the senators as to take laws from a citizen of Setia, he would enter the senate-house sword in hand, and slay with his own arm whatever Latin he saw.—Lib. vii. 5.

The purpose of this chapter has been to reconcile, what has been attempted but never achieved, *ut* with the subjunctive introducing *an actually accomplished fact*, and *ut* with the subjunctive expressing an *unfulfilled purpose*. If it be correct, as has hitherto been commonly believed, that the indicative is the mood of fact, and the subjunctive the mood of conception, the inevitable and irresistible conclusion is, that these two separate usages of the subjunctive are inconsistent and irreconcilable. It has, however, been proved in this chapter, that the expression of fact belongs to the subjunctive as well as to the indicative, if the fact be of a peculiar kind. *The expression of an extraordinary fact belongs to the subjunctive, just as the expression of a conception implying great probability, belongs to the indicative.* This partition of the province peculiar to each mood makes it quite clear that nothing is more natural or normal than that the subjunctive should express a fact, since the fact so expressed is always of a peculiar kind. This usage has been already shown to be in harmony with several other usages of the subjunctive. Its affinity to many others will appear more and more clear as this argument advances.

There are many apparent anomalies which become natural and normal when viewed in the light of the true theory of the subjunctive. It has been seen that *tantum* in the sense of "so great," and *tantum* in the sense of "so little," or "only," whichever meaning it may bear, is merely a deviation in a different direction from the same standard,—only so many degrees above or below it. And, as also has been seen, in either sense it is appropriately followed by the subjunctive.

In like manner, the usages of "primus," "ultimus," "solus," may be explained. The Romans said, primus, ultimus fecit, *i.e.*, he was the first or last to do it, but not primus vel ultimus fuit, qui faceret, as some might have supposed. The Romans by saying primus fecit, implied that he who did it was a forerunner who had many followers that did the same thing. In the same way by saying ultimus fecit, a Roman writer attracted attention to the great number who did the same thing before the last who did it.

On the other hand, the Latins by saying

Ille solus fuit, qui faceret—

expressed by all the emphasis of which their language was capable, that he who did so had no forerunner, no follower, but was his own great parallel.

According to the same principle the Romans wrote,—

*Una* est, quae *reparet*, seque ipsa *reseminet* Ales.
Haec *altera* victoria, quae cum Marathonia comparari
    *possit* tropaeo.
Erant omnino itinera *duo*, quibus domo exire *possent*.
                                In omnibus saeculis
*pauciores* viri reperti sunt, *qui* suas cupiditates, quam
    qui hostium copias, vincerent.—Cic.

*Quotus* enim *quisque* (*i.e.*, how few) philosophorum invenitur, qui *sit* ita moratus, ut ratio postulat?—Cic., *Tus.*, ii. 4.

Raros equis insidentes, *raros*, *quibus* ferrum in manu *sit* invenies.—Livy, viii. 38.

Tu *unus eximius* es, in *quo* hoc praecipuum ac singulare *valeat?*—*Id.*, ix. 34.

Itaque, postquam inter multas sententias *una*, *quae*, omissa cura communium, ad respectum suarum quemque rerum, *avertisset*, audita cuncti eam sententiam ingenti assensu accepere.—*Id*, ix. 45.

# CHAPTER VI.

### THE FUNCTION OF *QUUM*.

Of all the particles in the Latin language which are used with the indicative or the subjunctive, according to the meaning to be expressed, there is none between whose usages with these two moods, there is a greater difference, than between the usages of *quum*. The function of *quum* with the indicative is either to point out with precision the date of an event,—*e. g.*

Camillus meliore multo laude, quam *cum* triumphantem albi per urbem *vexerant* equi, insignis justitia fideque, hostibus victis, in urbem rediit.—Livy, v. 28.

Or to point out the simple coincidence between two ordinary events,—*e. g.*

*Legebam* tuas epistolas, *quum* mihi epistola *affertur* a Lepta.—Cic., *Att.*, ix. 12.

On the other hand, *quum* with the subjunctive, marks a coincidence between two events, which produced an *extraordinary* effect, and which the historian most fitly and forcibly expresses by the employment of that mood,—*e. g.*

Haec atque alia eodem pertinentia seditiosus

atque facinorosus homo, hisque artibus domi opes nactus, *cum maxime dissereret*, intervenit Tarquinius. —Livy, i. 50.

The entrance of the Roman Tarquin into the council chamber of the Latin chiefs, at the very time that Turnus of Aricia was inveighing against him with all the severity of savagery, was certainly an extraordinary coincidence. Nor was the consequence less extraordinary. The lips of Turnus were instantly sealed in silence. *Is finis orationi fuit.*

The usage of *quum* causal with the subjunctive is not less striking than the usage of *quum* temporal. It has nothing in common with *quod*, *quia*, and *quoniam*, all of which are properly joined with the indicative, and assign a reason for an ordinary fact, without condition, qualification, or reserve. This will best be proved in connexion with the well-known, but not well-understood phrase, *Quae cum ita sint*, the common, though, of course, not correct interpretation of which is "This being the case," or "Since this is the case." That would be a correct interpretation of *Rebus se ita habentibus*, but not of *Quae cum ita sint*. There is nothing in the interpretation thus given which bears any affinity to the idea which the Romans associated with the subjunctive. What is the true interpretation of the phrase will be seen by a consideration of its context in Cæsar. In a conference with the ambassadors of the Swiss, Cæsar had said:—

Quod si veteris contumeliae oblivisci vellet, num etiam recentium injuriarum, quod eo invito per provinciam per vim tentassent, quod Aeduos, quod Ambarros, quod Allobrogas, vexassent, memoriam deponere posse? and then he added, *Quum ea ita sint* tamen, si obsidis ab iis sibi dentur, uti ea quae polliceantur facturos intelligat, sese cum iis pacem facturum esse ; *i. e.*, The Swiss had aggravated their original offence against the Romans by the commission of other offences against their allies, and at last added one more against the authority of Caesar himself; but still, he said, *Quum ea ita sint*, *i. e.*, although these things are so, are what they *ought not* to be, are what I did not expect, yet on the fulfilment of certain conditions, I will make peace with you.

This usage of *quum* with the subjunctive, introducing something which is strange, or exceptional, or wrong, is quite in accordance with what has been seen to be the true character of that mood in a preceding chapter. Two similar usages may be given from Livy :—

Qui terrores, *cum* compescere *deberent*, auxere insuper animos plebis.—ii. 43.

*Quum* with the subjunctive—*deberent*—implies that the alarms introduced in the preceding clause, instead of allaying, as they might have been *expected*, and *ought* to have done, only exasperated the feelings of the commoners.

The other passage is as follows :—

Missi tamen feciales: nec eorum, *cum* more patrum jurati *repeterent* res, verba sunt audita.—iv. 30.

*Quum* with the subjunctive—*repeterent*,—implies, that though the heralds did not succeed in getting satisfaction, yet, inasmuch as they had taken the oath, and proceeded in a constitutional manner, they *ought* to have succeeded.

*Quum* is closely connected in etymology with *qui*, just as ὡς in Greek is closely connected with ὅς. Nor is the affinity between their usages with the subjunctive less close and certain. *Qui* is appropriately joined to the subjunctive when it introduces some *exceptional or extraordinary* distinction, *e. g.*— Caninius mirifica fuit vigilantia, *qui* suo toto consulatu somnum non *viderit.*—Cic. *ad Fam.*, vii. 30. So is *quum* joined with the subjunctive, when it introduces something *exceptional* or *extraordinary*. It was thus that T. Manlius, the consul, colleague of Decius, addressed his son :—

Sed *quum* aut morte tua sancienda *sint* consulum imperia, *aut impunitate in perpetuum abroganda:* nec te quidem, si quid in te nostri sanguinis est, recusare censeam, quin disciplinam militarem, culpa tua prolapsam, poena restituas. I, lictor, deliga ad palum.

But seeing that the authority of the consuls must either be upheld by your death, or annulled for ever by your exemption from punishment, I could not believe that even you should refuse, if any of my blood is in your veins, to restore by your punishment, the military subordination, which has been impaired by your disobedience.—Livy, viii. 7.

The two extreme alternatives are here fully and forcibly introduced by *quum*.

The next passage, also from Livy, is equally striking:—

Ceterum, qui de plebe allegebantur, *juxta* eam rem *aegre* passi patres, quam *quum* consulatum vulgari *viderent*.

But, because the augurs were being chosen from the commoners, the patricians experienced the same mortification at that event as when they saw the monopoly of the consulship destroyed. x. 6.

What were the feelings of the proud patricians, when they saw the consulship which they had prized as their own peculiar possession for upwards of one hundred and fifty years, pass into the hands of poor plebeians, it is not difficult to divine. Roman patricians then, like British peers lately, when the Reform Bill was about to pass, predicted that the sun of their country's greatness was soon to set. It is no exaggeration, then, to say, that *quum* joined with the subjunctive—*viderent*—introduces an *extraordinary* event.

Two other illustrative instances of this usage of *quum* introducing something extraordinary or exceptional, will suffice. They are taken from Nepos. The first is:—

Cujus ratio etsi non valuit, tamen magnopere est laudanda, *quum amicior omnium libertati*, quam *suae fuerit dominationi*.

Although his policy was not successful, yet it is deserving of very great praise, since it was more favourable to the freedom of all than his own absolute supremacy.—*Mil.* iii.

Consideration for the interests of others, to the exclusion of their own, was certainly not a common characteristic of Athenian statesmen or Grecian states. In the next biography the Spartans are censured for the opposite propensity:—

Lacedaemonios autem male et injuste facere, qui id potius intuerentur, quod *ipsorum dominationi*, quam quod *universae Graeciae utile* esset.—*Them.* vii.

So conspicuous an instance of disinterested policy on the part of Miltiades, so contrary to what was common in Greece, is fitly and forcibly described by the subjunctive.

The passage which contains the remaining illustrative instance is:—

Id quantae saluti fuerit universae Graeciae, bello cognitum est Persico, *quum* Xerxes et mari et terra bellum universae *inferret* Europae cum *tantis* copiis, *quantas neque antea, neque postea quisquam habuit.*

What safety that brought to the whole of Greece was discovered in the Persian war, when Xerxes, both by land and sea, made war on the whole of Europe, with such a force as none either before or since ever had.—*Them.* ii.

But the most remarkable usage of *quum* with the subjunctive, and one of the most remarkable of any usage whatever of that mood, still remains to be given. By it the marvellous mechanism of the Latin language is illustrated with great beauty and power. Sentences containing exemplifications of this usage have indeed already been selected and cited by critics, yet their peculiar scope and force have entirely escaped their observation. One of the most certain and conspicuous of these is cited by Crombie in his *Gymnasium*:—

*Quum* civitas armis jus suum exequi *conaretur,* Orgetorix mortuus est.—Cæs., *B. G.* iv.

And this sentence is supposed to be an illustration of the generalization:—

" *Quum,* when joined to a secondary clause, expressing a past action or event, as in progression, to which another action or event in the primary clause is expressed as contemporary, is joined with the subjunctive mood. In this sense it is nearly synonymous with *dum.*"—*Ed.* v., p. 85.

The supposition that *quum,* in the sentence cited from Cæsar, is "nearly synonymous with *dum,*" is a great delusion. Such sentences are so frequent as to be found in almost every page of many Latin writers, yet *dum* is not to be found forming a part of any of them. Before the proper relation between the two clauses in the sentence referred to can be seen, it will be necessary to consider the context in connexion with them :—

Orgetorix ad judicium familiam suam ad hominum milia decem conduxit; per eos ne causam diceret se eripuit. *Quum* ob eam rem incitata armis exequi *conaretur*, Orgetorix mortuus est, neque abest suspicio, quin ipse sibi mortem consciverit.

Orgetorix led to court his entire retinue of retainers, through whose instrumentality he freed himself from the necessity of pleading his case. When the state, exasperated at this act, was *attempting* to enforce its rights, Orgetorix died, and there existed ground for surmising that he had committed suicide.

*Quum* here with the subjunctive—*quum* jus exsequi *conaretur*—introduces an attempt about to become an actual fact, when suddenly and unexpectedly an obstacle occurs—Orgetorix mortuus est—to prevent its accomplishment. This is no solitary instance. Similar sentences, with a complete coincidence of circumstance, are found in sufficient numbers to justify the general conclusion that *quum* with the subjunctive, in accordance with the other usages of that mood, is employed to *introduce an attempt about to become an actual fact*, when an obstacle, *extraordinary* from its suddenness and unexpectedness, occurs to *prevent* its *accomplishment*. The following instances are adduced in demonstration of this conclusion:—

*Quum* jam in eo *esset*, ut oppido *potiretur*, procul in continenti lucus, qui ex insula conspiciebatur, *nescio quo casu*, nocturno tempore *incensus est*. Cujus flamma ut ab oppidanis et oppugnatoribus est visa, utrisque venit in mentem, signum a classiariis regiis datum. Quo factum est, ut et Parii a deditione deterrerentur et Miltiades timens, ne classis regia, adventaret, *incensis operibus, quae statuerat*, cum totidem navibus, atque erat profectus, Athenas magna cum offensione civium suorum *rediret.*

When he was now on the *eve* of gaining possession of the town, a grove at a great distance on the mainland, which was visible from the island, from some accident or other, I know not what, was set on fire during the night. No sooner was the flame seen than it occurred at once to the townspeople and the besiegers, that a signal had been given by the marines of the Persian king. The consequence was, that both the Parians were *prevented from surrendering,* and Miltiades, apprehensive that the king's fleet would arrive, having set fire to the works he had *commenced, returned* to Athens to the great displeasure of his countrymen.—Nep., *Mil.* vii.

Ad hoc consilium *quum* plerique *accederent,* Histiaeus Milesius, ne res *conficeretur, obstitit* dicens . . . . Hujus cum sententiam plurimi essent secuti, Miltiades, non dubitans, tam multis consciis ad regis aures consilia sua perventura, Chersonesum *reliquit,* ac rursus Athenas *demigravit.*

When the majority *were giving* their assent to this policy, Histiaeus of Miletus *opposed* the execution of the project, saying . . . . Most having adopted his views, Miltiades, not doubting, since so many were privy to them, that his proposals would reach the ears of the king, *left* the Chersonese, and again *returned* to Athens.—*Id.* iii.

Cujus fama perterriti classiarii quum manere non *auderent,* et plurimi *hortarentur,* ut domos suas quisque *discederent,* moenibusque se defenderet, Themistocles *unus restitit,* et universos pares esse posse, dispersos testabatur perituros. Barbarus ergo victus est magis consilio Themistoclis, quam armis Graeciae.

When the marines, panic-struck at the report of this event, had not the courage to keep their ground, and most of them were recommending that each should go home and defend himself within the walls of his native city, Themistocles alone opposed the proposal, and maintained that all together they would be a match for the foe, but if scattered they would be lost.—Nep., *Them.* iv.

Hic *quum* propter multas ejus virtutes magna cum dignitate *viveret,* Lacedaemonii *legatos Athenas miserunt,* qui eum absentem accusarent, quod societatem cum Persarum rege ad Graeciam opprimendam fecisset. Id ut audivit, Corcyram *demigravit.*

While here he was *beginning* to live with great consideration, because of his many excellent qualities, the Spartans *sent ambassadors* to Athens to *accuse him behind his back* of having made an alliance with the King of Persia for the overthrow of Greece. Themistocles, on hearing this, *removed* to Corfu.—*Id.*, viii.

In itinere, *quum* jam in eo *esset,* ut *comprehenderetur, ex vultu* cujusdam ephorum, qui eum admonere cupiebat, insidias sibi fieri intellexit. Itaque paucis ante gradibus, quam qui sequebantur, in aedem Minervae, quae χαλκιοικος, vocatur, confugit.

When he was now *on the eve of being arrested* on the road, from the *countenance* of one of the Spartan magistrates, who wished to warn him, he *perceived* that a plot was being laid for him. Accordingly, only a few steps in advance of those who followed him, he *found an asylum* in the temple of Minerva, the brazen one, as it is called.—Nep., *Paus.* v.

In this the last illustrative instance from Nepos, the phraseology—*Quum* jam in eo *esset, ut comprehenderetur*—is precisely the same as in the first instance from that author—*Quum* jam in eo *esset*, ut oppido potiretur.

In the sentences to be adduced from Livy, the peculiar combination of circumstances is not less complete and conclusive than in those that have been adduced from Cæsar and Nepos.

Eo tempore in regia prodigium visu eventuque mirabile fuit. Puero dormienti, cui Servio Tullio nomen fuit, caput arsisse ferunt in multorum conspectu. Plurimo igitur clamore inde ad tantae rei miraculum orto excitos reges : et, *cum* quidam familiarium aquam ad restinguendam *ferret*, ab regina *retentum :* sedatoque eam tumultu moveri vetuisse puerum, donec sua sponte expcrectus esset. Mox cum somno et flamman abiisse. Juvenis evasit vere indolis regiae : nec cum quaereretur gener Tarquinio, quisquam Romanae juventutis ulla arte conferri potuit: filiamque ei suam Rex despondit.

At that time a phenomenon, remarkable both in appearance and in its result, took place in the palace. The story goes that the head of the boy, whose name was Servius Tullius, when asleep, took fire, before the eyes of many. A loud cry, consequently, having been raised through wonder at so remarkable an event, the king and queen were thereby startled; and when one of the domestics *was bringing* water to quench the flame, he *was stopped* by the queen; who, after the uproar had ceased, forbad the boy to be stirred till he should awake of his own accord. Soon afterwards the fire and sleep left him together. He turned out a youth of truly princely tastes, and since no Roman could be compared with him in any accomplishment, when a son-in-law was sought for the king, on no other than him did Tarquin bestow the hand of his daughter.—Livy, i. 39.

His immortalibus editis operibus, *cum* ad exercitum recensendum concionem in campo ad Caprae paludem *haberet*, *subito* coorta tempestas cum magno fragore tonitribusque, tam denso regem *operuit* nimbo, ut conspectum ejus concioni abstulerit: nec deinde in terris Romulus fuit.

After the achievement of these imperishable works, when he *was preparing to hold a meeting* beside the marsh of Capra, for the purpose of reviewing the army, *all at once* a storm having arisen, accompanied by thunder and lightning, *enveloped the king in a cloud so thick* as to conceal him from mortal sight. Nor was Romulus any longer visible on earth.—*Id.*, i. 16.

Inter principia condendi hujus operis movisse numen ad indicandam tanti imperii molem traditur deos: nam, *cum* omnium sacellorum exaugurationes *admitterent* aves, in Termini fano non addixere.

During the commencement of the foundation of this work, it is recorded that the gods exerted their power in foreshadowing the extent of the mighty empire: for while the birds *were sanctioning* the desecration of all the other shrines, they *did not* give their sanction in the case of the temple of Terminus.—*Id.*, i. 55.

Romani, *quum* ad alias angustias protinus *pergerent*, saeptas, dejectu arborum saxorumque ingentium objacente mole *invenere*.

The Romans, when they *were proceeding straightway* to the other narrow pass, *found it blocked up* by felled trees and an opposing mass of huge stones.—*Id.*, ix. 2.

Consules profecti ad Pontium in colloquium, *quum* de foedere victor *agitaret*, *negarunt*, injussu populi foedus fieri posse.

The consuls having repaired to Pontius for a conference, while the conqueror *was making* proposals about a treaty, *denied* the possibility of making a treaty without the sanction of the people.—*Id.*, 5.

Et *quum* jam prope in portis castrorum *esset* hostis, nil consulto dictatore, magister equitum, Q. A. Cerretanus, magno tumultu cum omnibus turmis equitum evectus, *summovit* hostem.

And when by this time the enemy *was almost at the gate of the camp*, the master of the cavalry, Q. A. Cerretanus, without consulting the dictator at all, sallying forth with all his troops of horse, amid great confusion, *caused the foe to retire.—Id.*, 22.

Dum haec in Apulia gerebantur, altero exercitu Samnitis Interamnum, Coloniam Romanam, quae via Latina est, occupare conati, urbem non tenuerunt ; agros depopulati *quum* praedam aliam inde mixtam hominum atque pecudum, colonosque captos *agerent*, in victorem consulem *incidunt*, ab Luceria redeuntem : nec praedam solum amittunt, sedipsi longo atque impedito agmine incompositi caeduntur.

During these transactions in Apulia, the Samnites, with another army, having attempted to take possession of Interamnum, a Roman settlement, situated on the via Latina, did not reach the city ; but having devastated the adjacent territories, when they *were carrying* off other booty composed of men and cattle, and taking the colonists captive, they fell in with the victorious consul, on his return from Luceria : nor do they lose their booty only, but they themselves in a long obstructed line of march are slain in disorder.—*Id.*, 36.

It will be remembered that Crombie, in his "Gymnasium," as quoted above, has stated, "*Cum*, when joined to a secondary clause, expressing a past action or event, as in progression, to which another action or event, in the primary clause, is expressed as contemporary, is joined with the subjunctive mood. In this sense it is nearly synonymous with *dum*." It has already been remarked, that the author of the "Gymnasium" has altogether mistaken the conditions of the peculiar combination, which has been illustrated at so great length. His statement, that "*Quum* in this sense is nearly synonymous with *dum*," proves as much. In the passage just quoted from Livy, *dum* is found as well as *quum*, but with the greatest possible difference. That difference is well expressed by a difference of mood. In *the first* part of the passage Livy says,—

*Dum* haec in Apulia *gerebantur*, altero exercitu Samnites urbem non *tenuere*.

By *dum*, here, with the indicative, the coincidence between two ordinary events is simply expressed.

On the other hand, by *quum*, with the subjunctive, in the following combination, it is implied that *an attempt is about to become an actual fact, when suddenly and unexpectedly an obstacle interposes to prevent its accomplishment.*

*Quum agerent* praedam, in consulem *incidunt*, nec praedam solum *amittunt* sed etiam *caeduntur*.

The coincidence between this passage and another in the very first chapter of Livy is complete:—

*Quum*, Trojani ex agris praedam *agerent*, Latinus rex Aboriginesque ad *arcendam vim* advenarum armati ex urbe *concurrunt*.

It is somewhat remarkable that this beautiful usage of the subjunctive has never hitherto been pointed out, for the passage containing the erroneous generalization in the "Gymnasium," along with the passage from Cæsar, supposed to support it, has been quoted in a work already in its twenty-second edition, "Rudiments for the Edinburgh Academy."

The usage of *quum* with the plup. subjunctive, so frequently found in Latin, is the only one that remains to be explained. In the last chapter, a passage from Cæsar, along with five others, was adduced to prove, that the expression of fact belonged to the subjunctive as well as to the indicative. That passage contained a fact expressed by the plup. subjunctive:—

*Quum* Cæsari id nuntiatum *esset*, eos per provinciam nostram iter facere conari, maturat ab urbe proficisci, et quam maximis potest itineribus in Galliam ulteriorem contendit et ad Genevam pervenit. Provinciae toti quam maximum potest militum numerum imperat.—*De Bel. Gal.*, i. 7.

What is expressed by *nuntiatum esset* is a most undoubted fact, though expressed by the subjunctive. The extraordinary character of the fact, which is the cause of the subjunctive, is best seen by a consideration of its consequences. The intelligence that an enemy was cherishing the desire and contemplating the design of marching through a Roman dependency, caused Cæsar to *quit* the city to *hasten* to Geneva, and to *raise* the largest possible force. This fact, moreover, expressed by the subjunctive—*nuntiatum esset*,—being the cause and not the consequence of all the facts that follow, *so far from being dependent* on them, makes *them dependent* on it. Such entire strangers were the Romans to the modern doctrine of dependence.

Another sentence also already quoted from Cæsar, furnishes a most expressive usage of *quum* with the plup. subjunctive:

Gallis magno ad pugnam erat impedimento quod pluribus eorum scutis uno ictu pilorum transfixis et colligatis, *quum ferrum se inflexisset*, neque evellere neque sinistra impedita satis commode pugnare poterant; multi ut diu jactato brahio præoptarent scutum manu emittere et nudo corpore pugnare.—*Bel. Gal.*, i. 25.

The clause which first arrests attention in this sentence is, of course — *quum ferrum se inflexisset*. When once the point of the missile had bent itself, then followed the tugging and tossing of the left arm, and finally the fight with bare bodies.

The following sentences from Nepos combine the same condition and point to the same conclusion:—

Nam *quum* virtute militum hostium *devicisset* exercitus, summa aequitate res constituit, atque ipse ibidem manere decrevit.—*Mil. 2.*

The first and most formidable task Miltiades had to charge himself with was the subjugation of his enemies. This done, what followed was easy enough.

Hujus *quum* sententiam plurimi *essent* secuti, Miltiades non dubitans, tam multis consciis, ad regis aures consilia sua perventura, Chersonesum reliquit, ac rursus Athenas demigravit.—*Id.*, 3.

The resolution to oppose the policy proposed by Miltiades produced a rapid and remarkable revolution in the Chersonese—the immediate resignation of his post and return to Athens.

The language of Livy in connexion with *quum* and the plup. subjunctive could not have been more conclusive, though he had been writing a treatise on the true theory of the subjunctive. So usually, if not uniformly, is the combination in question found in the description of *extraordinary* occasions:—

Et *quum* (quod *per magnos tumultus* fieri solitum erat) justitio indicto, delectus sine vacationibus *habitus esset*: legiones quantum maturari potuit, in Auruncos ductae.—vii. 28.

Here it is expressly stated that a levy had been made without exemption—*quum delectus sine vacatione habitus esset*—which only took place in the case of formidable insurrections.

Habere Samnites victoriam non praeclaram solum, sed etiam perpetuam: cepisse enim eos non Romam, sicut ante Gallos, sed quod multo bellicosius fuerit, Romanam virtutem ferociamque. Quum haec dicerentur audirenturque et *deploratum* paene Romanum nomen in concilio sociorum fidelium *esset*; dicitur, etc.—x. 6.

Here Livy, after having represented the Campanians to have said, that the Samnites had not, as the Gauls had done, taken Rome captive, but the valour of the Romans, crowns the climax himself by stating that the Roman name had almost been *looked on as lost* in an assembly of their allies. This climax is most forcibly and fitly expressed by *quum* with the plup. subjunctive:—*Quum deploratum* paene Romanum nomen in concilio sociorum fidelium *esset*.

# CHAPTER VII.

### THE ESSENTIAL UNITY OF THE SUBJUNCTIVE.

In the preceding chapters, usages of the subjunctive, apparently the most remote from each other, but actually closely and clearly related, have been adduced at considerable length. These all coming so far, yet converging at last to a common centre, cannot fail to carry conviction to every candid mind. Before proceeding to sum up the results of the preceding investigations, to submit a series of these very various usages, and to show the *essential unity* which *underlies* them all, one other usage must be examined in detail, remarkable alike for the clear and strong evidence it supplies to establish the theory advocated for the first time in these pages, and to demolish the theory hitherto advocated both by British and Continental scholars.

The usage here referred to is that of *priusquam* or *antequam* with the subjunctive. The deliverance of Professor Madvig of Copenhagen on this point is:—"Yet the imp. and pl. subjunctive are also employed in *simply* indicating a period of time, and an action which has really taken place (especially with *antequam, priusquam,* in the historical style)."— *Lat. Gram.,* p. 310.

The deliverance of Zumpt on this point is:— "*Antequam* and *priusquam* are commonly used in a narrative with the imp. and pl. subjunctive, *if there is some connexion between the preceding and the subsequent action;* but if the simple priority of one action to another is expressed, the indicative is used." —*Lat. Gram.,* p. 408.

This opinion of Zumpt, which bears a strong affinity to the "essential part" theory, has been adopted substantially by a name of no less note than that of the late J. W. Donaldson of Trinity College, Cambridge, a name of European as well as English repute :—

"*Antequam* and *priusquam* are used with the indicative when there is merely a mark of tense and no hypothetical connexion ; *but we have the subjunctive* when the preceding event is supposed to be in some sort the cause of the subsequent."— *Complete Lat. Gram.,* p. 152.

That a scholar like Dr Donaldson, conspicuous alike for his courage and capacity, whose writings, at the very first sight, put to flight any impression of intellectual impotence, and beyond almost any productions of his contemporaries, bear the impress of intellectual independence, should have allowed himself, where truth was concerned, to be tied by the trammels of tradition, should have accepted the old theory of the subjunctive, is a most remarkable fact.

It is all the more remarkable, because it cannot be said, that engaged with other themes, with which his name is intimately and imperishably associated, the syntax of the Latin language had escaped his more earnest observation. He made Latin syntax the subject of special study. But it will be most satisfactory to have his own testimony on this point.

"I am not acquainted with any Latin grammar, whether old or new, which does not exhibit a faulty arrangement of the materials, and which is not deformed more or less by grave mistakes, both of principle and of detail, and thus I have had a special reason for the present endeavour to supply the deficiency by my own exertions."

It will soon be seen from the best and strongest of all evidence, the evidence of the Latin writers themselves, that the "principle" of Dr Donaldson is as erroneous as that of any of his predecessors.

In the first book of Livy the following passage is found:—

Tarquinius in diem certam ut Latinorum proceres ad lucum Ferentinae conveniant, indicit. Ipse diem quidem servavit, sed paulo *ante, quam sol occideret* venit.—*Cap.* 50.

According to Professor Madvig, as quoted above, "*ante*" here joined with *occideret* "simply indicates a period of time, and an action which has really taken place." The learned Professor thus, in direct opposition to almost all other grammarians, assigns to *priusquam* with the subjunctive the same function as *priusquam* with the indicative. If the subjunctive only expresses the same as the indicative, what is the use of the subjunctive? It can only encumber without enriching the language. Everybody who knows anything at all about Latin, knows that there is a great difference between *dum, quum, quin, si, ut,* when used with the indicative, and when used with the subjunctive. Nor is the difference less between *priusquam* when used with the one mood, and when used with the other. Nothing is more remarkable about the Latin language than its logical consistency, although the different theories in vogue regarding its subjunctive have rendered it the most illogical language that ever was written.

According to Zumpt, since *antequam* is used with the subjunctive *occideret* in the passage under review, "there is some connexion between the preceding and subsequent action," *i.e.*, between *venit* and *occideret*, or, according to Donaldson, "the preceding event *venit* is supposed to be in some sort the cause of the subsequent *occideret*, *i.e.*, the arrival of Tarquinius was the cause of the setting of the sun! This will match anything that has ever been said or written about the "*predicate*" itself even.

It is now time to see what is the real cause of *antequam* being joined with the subjunctive *occideret*. The cause is found a few lines farther down in the narrative of Livy, who represents Turnus Herdonius, the political opponent of Tarquin thus speaking:—"*An quicquam superbius esse*, quam ludificari sic omne nomen Latinum? Principibus longe ab domo excitis, *ipsum, qui concilium indixerit,* non adesse: *i.e.,* Could anything be more insolent than thus to make game of the entire Latin nation? After that the chiefs had been summoned a great distance from their homes, the very man who had given notice of the convention was not himself present.

Livy, by employing the subjunctive *occideret* rather than the indicative *occidit,* implies that the conduct of Tarquin, under the circumstances, was both *strange* and *wrong.* The other members of convention were present at dawn of day—prima luce. This usage of the subjunctive bears a close and clear affinity to those already explained in this work, to *sunt qui dicant* for instance. The generalized form of Tarquinius paulo antequam sol *occideret,* venit, would be:—*Sunt qui* non promissa *servent.*

It so happens that the writings of Livy, equally luminous and voluminous, furnish an instance of *priusquam* and *sol* joined with the indicative, so that the proof of the truth of the interpretation just given is perfect and complete:—

*Aliquamdiu* utrimque intenti steterunt, expectantes ut ab adversariis clamor et pugna inciperet: et *prius sol meridie* se inclinavit, *quam* telum hinc aut illinc *emissum est.*—Lib. ix. 32.

The time that the one foe waited for the other to begin the battle, was not from morn till dewy eve, *prima luce—sol occideret—*as in the preceding case, but only a considerable time—*aliquamdiu—*before noon. Had they waited till near sunset, Livy would have written *emitteretur*.

Out of many more, one other sentence may be given, which shows how utterly incorrect in fact, and unsound in principle, and to what absurd consequences it leads, the belief of those who suppose that the idea associated by the Romans with the subjunctive was that of "connexion," or "cause," or "complement of a clause," or "dependence":—

Ducentis annis *ante quam* Romam *caperent* in Italiam Galli transcenderunt.—Arnold's *Latin Prose Composition*. Part i., p. 151.

Surely the "connexion between the preceding action"—the crossing of the Alps—"and the subsequent one"—the capture of Rome—cannot be very close, since the two acts were divided by an interval of two hundred years. The subject is too ludicrous for grave discussion. It was better in Arnold (*Nepos*, p. 128) to have said of the relation of such clauses, "there is no closer connexion than mere priority of time, or if any, it is extremely slight," than to give an explanation which only stultifies the Roman writers, and mystifies their meaning. Whenever the sense of this sentence, and similar ones, is made clear, then the reason of the syntax will also appear. As Rome was not built in one day, so it was not captured in one day. An enterprise of such an extent would require great experience, and the expenditure of *extraordinary* effort. Nothing, therefore, is more natural than that the historian, in describing the event, should employ the subjunctive.' There is another sentence in Virgil almost precisely parallel, with the same sense, and, of course, the same syntax :—

> Principio, *Italiam*, quam tu jam rere propinquam,
> Vicinosque, ignare, paras invadere portus,
> Longa procul longis via dividit invia terris.
> *Ante* et Trinacria tentandus remus in unda,
> Et salis Ausonii lustrandum navibus aequor,
> Infernique lacus, Aeaeaeque insula Circae,
> *Quam* tuta *possis* urbem componere terra.—
>
> Æn., iii. 380.

Only four more sentences containing *priusquam* with the subjunctive will be given, each of which contains the common characteristic of some *extraordinary* or *exceptional* circumstance.

*Interfuit* autem pugnae navilis apud Salamina, quae facta est *priusquam* poena *liberaretur*.—Nep., *Ar.* ii.

Aristides, who had been sentenced to banishment for ten years, was freed from punishment, not by the expiry of that period, but by a remission of a portion of his sentence, which enabled him to be present at the battle of Salamis. This *exceptional* act is appropriately expressed by *priusquam liberaretur*.

It will be remembered that in the fourth chapter of this work, an extract from Livy was given detailing the circumstances of the base betrayal of Tib. Gracchus, by a base Lucanian, into the hands of his enemies. Some time before he left Lucania, as it turned out, to meet his terrible doom, a remarkable phenomenon presented itself to him, which seemed to the soothsayers to foreshadow what was soon to follow. The historian marks his sense of the extraordinary event by the employment of the subjunctive:—

Graccho, *priusquam* ex Lucanis *moveret*, sacrificanti, triste prodigium factum est. ad exta, sacrificio perpetrato, augues duo, ex occulto allapsi, edere jecur conspectique repente ex oculis abiere. Id quum aruspicum monitu sacrificium instauraretur, atque intentius exta reservarentur; iterum ac tertium venisse tradunt, libatoque jocinore intactos angues abiisse. Quum aruspices, ad imperatorem id pertinere prodigium, praemonuissent, et ab occultis cavendum hominibus consultisque; nulla tamen providentia fatum imminens moveri potuit.—Lib. xxv. 17.

The following sentence furnishes a similar instance of a premonitory prodigy, which is fitly, of course, expressed by the subjunctive:—*Ante* paucis *quam occideret* mensibus, cornix in capitolio elocuta est.—*Suet.*

In the next and last illustrative instance of *priusquam* with the subjunctive, the employment of that mood expresses wonder and censure at the indecent haste with which the burning of the dead had been performed,—Puer ante noctem mortuus est, et postridie *priusquam liceret*, combustus est.—*Cic.*

Before giving finally a combined view of all the usages of the subjunctive, it has been deemed desirable to contrast a few sentences containing the subjunctive and indicative respectively.

In one of his letters Cicero says,—Gaudeo quod *redieris incolumis.* The subjunctive of course is used, because his friend had returned safe and sound from amid great dangers.

On the other hand, Cicero also says,—Gaudeo, quod bene *vales.* The indicative of course is used, because his friend is in his usual state of good health. The clause containing the indicative in this sentence is as much dependent as the clause in the preceding sentence containing the subjunctive. The two clauses are quite on an equality in this respect; hence the consideration which determined the mood was the character of the circumstance described.

Again, Horace says,—

        Non hercule miror
  Aiebat, si qui *comedunt* bona.

Here the indicative is used, because it expresses a fact at which Horace did not wonder.

On the other hand, Cicero says,—*Mirabile* videtur, quod non *rideat* haruspex, quum haruspicem viderit. Here the subjunctive is used, because it expresses a fact at which Cicero *does wonder.*

But the following sentence from Livy contains in close contiguity, and places in striking contrast, one clause with the subjunctive, and another with the indicative:—

Quo praesidio *quum fulta* res Romana *esset, levius*

*fuit*, quod Gallos mox Praeneste venisse, atque inde circa Pedum consedisse, *auditum est.*—Lib. vii. 12.

In the first clause the subjunctive is used most appropriately, because the Romans had received a large reinforcement of soldiers from the Latins, a help quite *extraordinary*, for Livy expressly says in the preceding sentence—quod multis intermiserant annis—*i.e.*, had discontinued sending for many years. On the other hand, the indicative is used in the second clause, because it introduces a fact of comparatively little importance—*levius fuit quod*.

The first of a long list of sentences exhibiting *the essential unity underlying all the usages* of the subjunctive, contains a usage of that mood with *Si*. Since it has been proved in the preceding pages that the essential idea which the Romans associated with the subjunctive was that of *difference from a common standard, whether in the direction of excess or defect*, it follows as a corollary, that *Si* with the subjunctive will express what is *improbable*, which is the *very reverse* of what Grotefend laid down, as will be seen by a reference to the second chapter of this work. This first illustrative sentence with *Si* also contains two other instances of the subjunctive, expressing of course the same idea,—an idea so familiar to the Roman writers, that hardly anything can appear less forced or far-fetched than its inference from their works.

1. Humano capiti cervicem pictor equinam
   Jungere *si velit* et varias inducere plumas

Undique collatis membris, *ut* turpiter atrum
*Desinat* in piscem mulier formosa superne,
Spectatum admissi *risum teneatis* amici?
—Hor., *A. P.* 1.

*Quasi*, a compound of *Si*, and expressing an idea similar to that expressed by *Si* in the preceding sentence, is followed by the same mood:—

II. Proinde *quasi* nostram ipsam mentem videre possimus.—Sen., *Mil.* 31.

The explanation of the two apparently contrary meanings of *tantum*, "so much and so little," *i.e.*, "only," is found in the fact, that each is only the expression of an extreme, one above, the other below an ordinary standard, and both extremes meet in being expressed by the subjunctive. No single word in Latin exhibits so concisely and conclusively the true theory of the subjunctive.

III. Tantum (so much) favoris incussit, *ut* nemo causa pugnandi *restiterit.*—Livy, xxxvii. 21.

IV. Tantum (so few) repperit *ut* anguste xv. millia legionariorum militum transportare *possent.*—Cæs., *B. G.*, vi. 35.

This usage of *ut* with the subjunctive, introducing an actual fact, has hitherto been inexplicable, since the subjunctive has been regarded as the mood of conception. It has, however, been already proved in this work that the expression of fact belongs to the subjunctive as well as to the indicative, if of an extraordinary character, and since the facts introduced by *ut* in the two last sentences are of that character, that usage of *ut* with the subjunctive is as appropriate as it is in the following sentence, introducing an unfulfilled purpose.

v. Nonnulli pudore adducti, *ut* timoris suspicionem *vitarent*, remanebant.—Cæs., *B. G.*, 139.

*Ut* also with great beauty introduces an attempt about to become an accomplished fact, when an *extraordinary* obstacle occurs to prevent its accomplishment.

vi. Quum jam in eo esset, *ut* oppido *potiretur*, in continenti lucus, nescio quo casu, noctu incensus est. Cujus flamma ut ab oppidanis et oppugnatoribus visa est, utrisque venit in opinionem, signum a classiariis regiis datum. Quo factum est ut Miltiades, *incensis operibus*, Athenas rediret.—Nep., *Mil.* 7.

The same idea is expressed with equal beauty by *quum* with the subjunctive.

vii. *Quum* haec maxime *dissereret*, *intervenit* Tarquinius. Is *finis orationis* fuit.

*Ut* also, like *tantum*, expresses *two extremes* with the subjunctive.

viii. Accidit (of evil fortune) *ut* una nocte omnes Hermae statuae *dejicerentur*.—Nep., *Al.* 3.

ix. Quod *nunquam opinatus fui*, id contigit (of *extreme* good fortune) *ut* salvi *potiremur* domum.—*Pl. Am.*, i. 1, 32.

That the idea inherent in the subjunctive is entirely *independent* of any preceding clause whatever, may be seen from the following additional usage of *ut* with the subjunctive:—

x. Egone ut te interpellem?—Cic., *Tus.*, ii. 18.

In the next two usages, not only is there no preceding clause, but there is no particle at all joined with the subjunctive.

xi. Injussu tuo, inquit, imperator, *extra ordinem nunquam pugnaverim.*—Livy, vii. 10.

xii. Quis *tulerit* Gracchos de seditione querentes.—*Juv.*

In both of these examples the idea implied in the subjunctive is repudiated as strange or wrong. This is equally the case with the two following:—

xiii. In medio *qui* Scripta foro *recitent, sunt* multi quique *lavantes.*—Hor.

xiv. Aristides nonne ob eam causam expulsus est patria, quod *praeter modum* justus *esset?*—Cic.

xv. Quae *quum* ita *sint.*—Caes. Although things are not as they ought to be.

xvi. Alexander, *quum* Clitum *familiarem* suum *interemissent,* manus a se vix abstinuit.—Cic., *Tus.,* iv. 37.

xvii. Non sum is, qui nubeculam tuae frontis *timeam.*—Cic. in *Pis.*

In the next instance there is an open expression of wonder at what is stated in the subjunctive.

xviii. *Mirum, quantum* illi viro, nuntianti haec, fidei *fuerit.*—Livy, i. 16.

But whether there is any direct statement relative to the subjunctive, there is always some *exceptional* or *extraordinary* circumstance peculiar to it, which explains itself, as in the following additional illustrative instances:—

XIX. *Ante* paucis quam *occideret* mensibus, *cornix* in capitolio *elocuta est.*—Suet.

XX.         *Irae* altis urbibus ultimae
        Stetere causae, cur *perirent*
        Funditus.—Hor.

XXI. O utinam primis *arsisses* ignibus infans.
        —Ov., *Met.* viii. 500.

XXII. Caninius fuit *mirifica* vigilantia, qui suo toto consulatu *somnum non viderit.*—Cic.

XXIII. Si *dignum* crearitis, qui *secundus ab* Romulo *numeretur.*—Livy, i. 17.

XXIV. *Major* sum quam cui *possit* fortuna nocere.
        —Ov., *Met.* vi. 195.

XXV. Non me carminibus vincet nec Thracius
        Orpheus,
    Nec Linus, huic mater *quamvis*, atque huic *pater adsit.*—Virgil, *Ec.* iv. 56.

XXVI. Phocion fuit perpetuo pauper, *quum ditissimus* esse *posset.*—Nep., *Phoc.* i.

XXVII. *Soli* centum erant, qui creari patres *possent.* Livy, i. 8.

XXVIII. In omnibus saeculis *pauciores* viri reperti sunt, qui suas *cupiditates*, quam qui hostium copias *vincerent.*—Cic.

XXIX. Nec quisquam temporibus illis *exstat*, quo satis certo auctori *stetur.*—Livy, viii. 40.

XXX. Quae latebra est, in quam *non intret* metus mortis?—Senec.

Instead of "Nullum quod tetigit non ornavit," part of Johnson's epitaph on Goldsmith, in Westminster Abbey, Cicero, Livy, and Catullus would have written :—

 xxxi. Nullum tetigit, quod non *ornaret*.

Many more sentences containing a similar characteristic might be added, were it not that the addition might only lengthen the illustration without strengthening the demonstration. Probably the sentences already adduced are such in number and nature as to suffice for proving that the true theory of the subjunctive represents it as expressing something *exceptional* or *extraordinary*. This theory the author believes to be as new as true. Assuredly he has never seen the slightest trace or hint of it anywhere else. If it had existed before, the different theories disposed of in this treatise would never have been conceived or believed. Its existence is incompatible with theirs. It summarily supersedes them by swallowing them up, like the rod of Aaron.

Jamque opere exacto, the author may write with more propriety than at the close of his first attempt:—

 Sed nos immensum spatiis confecimus aequor
 Et jam tempus equum fumantia solvere colla.

FINIS.

www.ingramcontent.com/pod-product-compliance
Lightning Source LLC
Chambersburg PA
CBHW031833230426
43669CB00009B/1334